IMAGES
of America

STANDING ROCK SIOUX

STANDING ROCK SIOUX TRIBAL FLAG. The flag of the Standing Rock Sioux is light blue with the tribal seal in the center. The seal's outer ring is white, edged by two narrow red bands, and reads, in red letters, "Standing Rock Sioux Tribe" above and "July 1873" below. This date is when the reservation was established. The seal contains a circle of eight white tipis representing the eight districts on the reservation. The ring of tipis encloses an inner yellow circle depicting the Standing Rock in white and outlined in red. The rock rests on a red pedestal. Around the edge of the yellow circle are the names of the eight districts in red. They include: Fort Yates, Cannon Ball, Wakpala, Kenel, Little Eagle, Bear Soldier, Rock Creek, and Porcupine. The tribal flag was presented to the author Donovin Sprague by members of the Standing Rock Sioux. Just recently the tribe adopted the original name of Long Soldier (Akicita Hanska) to replace the name of Fort Yates District. The city of Fort Yates is now in Long Soldier District. (Photograph courtesy of Donovin Sprague.)

IMAGES
of America

STANDING ROCK SIOUX

Donovin Arleigh Sprague

ARCADIA
PUBLISHING

Published by Arcadia Publishing
Charleston, South Carolina

Library of Congress Catalog Card Number: 2004100865

For all general information contact Arcadia Publishing at:
Telephone 843-853-2070
Fax 843-853-0044
E-mail sales@arcadiapublishing.com
For customer service and orders:
Toll-Free 1-888-313-2665

Visit us on the Internet at www.arcadiapublishing.com

Dedicated with love to Darrel, Velda, and Deb Sprague

CONTENTS

ACKNOWLEDGMENTS

My special thanks and appreciation go to everyone who helped me in this project. Thank you for photos, interviews, friendship, generosity, and conversation to all, past and present: Special thanks to my assistant Rylan Sprague for transferring photos to discs.

Bill and Geraldine Anderson, Paula Anderson Family, Ethel Bates and Family, Terry Bear Ribs, Mildred Benway, Jack Bickel, Gladys Bird Horse, Black Hills State University, Doyle Bramhall, Eddie Brigati, Robert Buffalo Boy Sr., Earl Bull Head, Jim Byington, Albert Cadotte, Jolene Cadotte, Judy Cadotte, Tyrone Cadotte, Pete and Cindy Catches, Cheyenne River Sioux Tribe, Jay Citron, Eddy Clearwater, Marie Cloud, Clown Family, Frank Conlin Gallery, Crazy Horse (Tasunke Witko) family descendants, Denver Public Library, Lisa Dowhaniuk, Germaine Archambault Eagle, Charmayne Eagleman, Oliver Eagleman, Fabulous Thunderbirds, Wilbur Flying By, Winona Flying Earth, Fort Phil Kearny-Wyoming, Chester Fuhrman Jr., Billy Gibbons, Samantha Gleisten, Sissy Goodhouse, Bill Green, Renee Greenman, Bill Groethe, Merle Haggard, Ted Harvey, Gladys Hawk, Mike and Nicole He Crow, Darlene Helper, Pete Helper, Matt Hennies, Theresa "TJ" Heying, Ray Higheagle, Mark Holman, Agatha Holy Bull, Hump Family, Iowa State University, Frank Jamerson, Waylon Jennings and Jessi, Don Jones, Sidney and Shirley Keith, Emory Dean Keoke, Diane Kindt, B.B. King, KLND-FM Standing Rock and Cheyenne River, Klein Museum-Mobridge, S.D., Carole Kloss, Jimmy D. Lane, Jonny Lang, Ernie and Sonja LaPointe, Marcella Ryan LeBeau, Bob Lee, Carol Lehrkamp, Little Bighorn National Monument, Avis Little Eagle, Thom Little Moon, Kevin Locke, Ethel Long Elk, Sis Lewis and Family, David and Joanie Lindley, Leonard Little Finger, Merle Lofgren, Barbara Logan, Lone Horn descendants, Clement Long, Longbrake Family, Alex Looking Elk, T.W. Lopez, Carideo and Estherlene Low Dog, Marie Many Wounds, Ruby Marshall, "McLaughlin Messenger", Ron McNeil His Horse Is Thunder, Berneita Miller and Family, Michael Moore, Michael Martin Murphey, Jim Nelson, Kathy Nelson, Willie Nelson, Daryl and Sharon No Heart, Byron Olson, Bob and Nell Pearson, Daren J. Pleets, Wilbur "Banny" Pleets, Pooley Family, Susan Kelly Power, Susan Mary Power, Marcie, Todd and Dylan Pudwill, Monique Rainbow, Cheryl Red Bear, Dollie Red Elk, Irwin Richardson, Rock N Records, Jimmy Rogers, Alvina "Lucille" Runs After, Junior Rousseau, Grover Scott, Dennis, Lila, Doren, and Darrel Serfling, Seven Council Fires, Shakedown, Tommy Shannon, Linda Sharff, Mark Shillingstad, Charles Shoots The Enemy, Harold Shunk, Siksika Nation-Alberta, Canada, Sitting Bull College, Catherine Brings The Horses Silva, Nancy Sinatra, Elsie Slides Off, the Smithsonian Institute, Brandon Sprague, Linda Stampoulos, Standing Rock Sioux Tribe, State Historical Society of North Dakota, Ken Stewart, Pamela Ternes, "Teton Times", Timber Lake and Area Historical Society, "Timber Lake Topic", Edith Traversie, Ben Trent, Mike Trent Family, Tribal Historic Preservation Office, Lorna Two Bears, Matt and Nellie Two Bulls, University of California, University of Iowa, University of Northern Iowa, University of South Dakota, Anne Valandra, Stevie Ray Vaughan, Renee Vermillion, Wakan Tanka, Claudette Walking Elk, Whitecap Dakota First Nation-Saskatchewan, Canada, Blanche White Eagle, Lois White Eagle, Melvin White Eagle, Sidney Whitesell Family, Kim Wilson, Mary Louise Defender Wilson, Wood Mountain Reserve-Canada, Wounded Knee Survivors Association, Yankton Sioux Tribe, Waste Win Young, Ed Young Man Afraid Of His Horses, Tom Zerr, ZZ Top.

INTRODUCTION

AKICITA HANSKA "LONG SOLDIER" AND INYAN WOSLATA "STANDING ROCK" SIOUX HISTORY

The Standing Rock Indian Reservation is located in south central North Dakota and in north central South Dakota. The tribe includes the bands of the Hunkpapa and Siha Sapa of the Lakota Nation, and the Hunkpatinas and Cuthead bands of the Dakota Nation, and Yanktonai grouped under the Nakota. The Cuthead band also belongs to the Upper Yanktonais and the Hunkpatinas are the Lower Yanktonais, who reside here.

The name Sioux is part of the Ojibwe/Ojibway/Chippewa/Anishinabe word "Nadoweisiw-eg," which the French shortened to Sioux. The original word meant "little or lesser snakes/enemies." The Sioux are really three groups comprised of the Lakota, Dakota, and Nakota, each having slightly different language dialects. Older dialects may have been lost including a "J" dialect used by some people in the area. The seven Lakota groups are the Hunkpapa, Siha Sapa, Minnicoujou, Itazipco, Oohenumpa, Oglala, and the Sicangu. The Hunkpapa and Siha Sapa are at Standing Rock Reservation. The Siha Sapa are in the southern part of the reservation on the South Dakota side, and Siha Sapa members continue into the Cheyenne River Indian Reservation which borders Standing Rock on the south. The Cheyenne River Indian Reservation is home to the Minnicoujou, Itazipco, Siha Sapa, and Oohenumpa. The Oglala are located at the Pine Ridge Indian Reservation in southern South Dakota, and the Sicangu are located at Rosebud Indian Reservation and Lower Brule Indian Reservation. Rosebud is in southern South Dakota just east of Pine Ridge, and Lower Brule is in central South Dakota. Some of the Lakota also settled in the Wood Mountain Reserve area in Saskatchewan, Canada.

The Yanktonais, Hunkpatinas, and Cuthead bands reside on the North Dakota side of the Standing Rock Indian Reservation. They are grouped under the Dakota and Nakota dialect groups and are not Lakota in category but are relatives. There has been intermarriage between bands and the Lakota/Dakota/Nation should be considered related. The Cannon Ball River is a tributary of the Missouri River and flows along the northern boundary of the reservation with the communities of Cannon Ball, Solen, Breien, and Shields-Porcupine located along the river, all on the North Dakota side. As you travel southwest the Cannon Ball becomes the Cedar River and the South Dakota communities located south of the Cedar include: McIntosh, Watauga, Morristown, Keldron, and Thunder Hawk. The Grand River also flows into the Missouri River, and communities near the Grand River include: Little Eagle and Bullhead in South Dakota.

North of the Grand River near the state line is Walker and McLaughlin, South Dakota. The eastern boundary of the reservation is the Missouri River and the communities on or near this river include: Fort Yates, N.D., Kenel, S.D., Mahto, S.D., Wakpala, S.D., and Mobridge, S.D. Mobridge is across the river, off the reservation. Selfridge, N.D. is west of Fort Yates. On the south end of the reservation most of these communities were or are on original Cheyenne River Reservation land, and these communities include Trail City, Glencross, Firesteel, Timber Lake, Isabel, and Glad Valley, all in South Dakota.

Standing Rock Indian Reservation tribal members are proud ancestors or family members who participated in every major event in early Lakota/Dakota/Nakota history including the recorded arrival of the French explorers Verendrye Brothers in the early 1700s in present South Dakota; Lewis and Clark Expedition in 1804; 1811–1812 Fort Manuel built; 1851 and 1868 Fort Laramie Treaty conferences; Minnesota Conflict of 1862; 1866 Fetterman Fight; 1866 Battle of Killdeer Mountain; 1867 Wagon Box Fight; 1867 Hayfield Fight; 1874 Custer Expedition into the Black Hills; 1874 Standing Rock Agency naming; 1876 Battle of the Rosebud; 1876 Battle of the Little Bighorn; 1876 Slim Buttes Fight; 1876–1877 Trek to Canada; September 5, 1877 Crazy Horse killing at Fort Robinson; 1877 Allotment Act and Reservation Period; 1878 Fort Yates establishment; 1889 Act to Divide the Great Sioux Reservation; 1890 Ghost Dance era and Sitting Bull killing; 1890 Wounded Knee Massacre; 1924 Indian Citizenship Act; 1934 Indian Reorganization Act; 1946 Indian Claims Commission; 1950s Termination and Relocation Acts/era; 1968 Indian Civil Rights Act; 1972 to today—Indian Self Determination and Educational Assistance era; 1978 Indian Religious Freedom Act and Indian Child Welfare Act; and the 1988 Indian Gaming Act.

Akicita Hanska "Long Soldier" was an early community at Inyan Woslata (Standing Rock) long before the arrival of the military and the establishment of Fort Yates. Akicita Hanska "Long Soldier" is where the city of Fort Yates is today and would be where the fort was built. Much of the written history about the area begins with the establishment of Fort Yates, without recognizing the Akicita Hanska "Long Soldier" community. When the military arrived there was already a plotted town and the inhabitants included the Hunkpapa, Yanktonai, Siha Sapa, Minnicoujou, and even Oglalas. When the military took the Census of 1876 the Yanktonai outnumbered everyone. The Yanktonai are also located with the Yankton Sioux at the Yankton Sioux Reservation and some at Crow Creek Reservation in South Dakota. People at Standing Rock, Yankton, and Crow Creek also have family ties to Fort Peck Reservation in Montana. Furthermore, Dakota tribes throughout eastern South Dakota, North Dakota, Minnesota, and Canada often have family connections. Fort Yates became the largest town on the reservation because of the military being based there. It served as a good river port.

Photographers contributed much to the history of this area and the best known were D.F. Barry and Frank B. Fiske. The author visited the State Historical Society of North Dakota whose archives house over 7,000 Fiske photos, many from Standing Rock. Many ended up with families as photos or postcards. Fiske arrived at Standing Rock in 1889 and later set up studios there and in Bismarck, N.D. Unpublished photos which the author presents include the collection of Oscar Huettner of Mobridge, S.D. and Frank Cundill from the Isabel/Timber Lake, S.D. area. Cundill's photos have seen very little book publication and Huettner's appear here for the first time.

Donnie Sprague
Cankahu Wankatuya (High Back Bone/Hump)
December 2003

One

OYATE
(PEOPLE/NATION)

LEGEND OF STANDING ROCK. The Standing Rock and legend has its origin with the Arikara (also called The Ree) tribe of North Dakota. There is possibly another original Standing Rock besides the one on display today. The following legend is by Marie L. McLaughlin: A Dakota had married an Arikara woman and by her had one child. By and by he took another wife. The first wife was jealous and pouted. When time came for the village to break camp she refused to move from her place on the tent floor. The tent was taken down but she sat on the ground with her babe on her back. The rest of the camp with her husband went on.

At noon her husband halted the line. "Go back to your sister-in-law," he said to his two brothers. "Tell her to come on and we will await you here. But hasten, for I fear she may grow desperate and kill herself."

The two rode off and arrived at their former camping place in the evening. The woman still sat on the ground. The elder spoke: "Sister-in-law, get up. We have come for you. The camp awaits you."

She did not answer and he put out his hand and touched her head. She had turned to stone!

The two brothers lashed their ponies and came back to camp. They told their story, but were not believed. "The woman has killed herself and my brothers will not tell me," said the husband. However, the whole village broke camp and came back to the place where they had left the woman. Sure enough, she sat there still, a block of stone!

The Indians were greatly excited. They chose out a handsome pony, made a new travois and placed the stone in the carrying net. Pony and travois were both beautifully painted and decorated

with streamers and colors. The stone was thought "wakan" (holy) and was given a place of honor in the center of the camp. Whenever the camp moved the stone and travois were taken along. Thus, the stone woman was carried for years and finally brought to Standing Rock Agency and now rests upon a brick pedestal in front of the Agency Office. From this stone Standing Rock Agency derives its name. There are other legends about the rock and one is that there was another rock which was a dog who was with the woman and child. This rock was lost, possibly in the stone in early construction of tribal buildings. Ella Deloria has some interesting stories about the rock in her book "Dakota Texts". (Undated photo from the Huettner Collection, courtesy of Klein Museum, Mobridge, S.D.)

RAIN IN THE FACE (HUNKPAPA). This photo was taken at Fort Keogh, Montana Territory, in 1880. Photographer L.A. Huffman photographed Rain In The Face following his return from Canada and his surrender to General Nelson Miles. (Copyright Jack Coffrin, Miles City, Montana. Postcard courtesy of Donovin Sprague.)

BLOODY MOUTH (HUNKPAPA). Bloody Mouth was a leader (Itancan) and member of Sitting Bull's band and was present with Sitting Bull at several raids and wars against white settlers and soldiers who overran Lakota/Dakota/Nakota hunting grounds. (Undated photograph taken by Gardner, courtesy of the Smithsonian Institute.)

MAD BEAR "MATO OSINSICA" (YANKTONAI).
Mad Bear was born in Minnesota near the
Mississippi in 1836. As a youth he was called
Watogle (Wild), and later as an adult was given the
name Mad Bear. He served as Itancan (Chief) of
the Mad Bear camp area of Standing Rock, which
consisted at one time of about 300 people. The
camp is now under water due to the construction
of the Oahe Dam on the Missouri River. Mad
Bear's father was Loud Thunder and his mother was
Black Lightning Woman. His brothers included
Elk, Crazy Bear, Walks In The Wind, Bobtail
Bear, Crow Feather, and Black Cloud. His sister
was Refina Mad Bear. Mad Bear's two wives were
sisters, Foremost Woman (also known as Leading
Woman) and Two Generations. Mad Bear was a
member of the Fool Soldier Band that rescued the
Shetak captives, who were white prisoners from
the Minnesota conflict of 1862. In the 1876 census
the Mad Bear tiwahe (family) is listed among the
Lower Yanktonai band. Mad Bear died in 1915
and is buried at Wakpala, S.D. The author knows
several descendants of Mad Bear and interviewed
Gladys Bird Horse (Oka), a great granddaughter
of the Chief. (Undated photo taken by D.F. Barry,
courtesy of the Smithsonian Institute.)

**LONG SOLDIER "AKICITA
HANSKA" (HUNKPAPA).** The
community district of Fort Yates
is named for Long Soldier. The
1885 census listed five family
members in his household.
(Undated photo by D.F.Barry,
courtesy of Donovin Sprague.)

11

YELLOW HAWK (LAKOTA/DAKOTA). This photo was taken at the Fiske studio in downtown Fort Yates, ND. Postcard developed by SHSND. (Undated photo taken by Frank Fiske, courtesy of Donovin Sprague.)

WHITE BEAR "MATO SKA" (YANKTONAI). White Bear was later known as Tom Frosted. In this photo he holds a rife and a beaded pipe bag lays on the floor. He has a robe wrapped around him and wears a deerskin shirt and eagle feather headdress. The White Bear family is listed among the Lower Yanktonais in the 1876 Standing Rock Census and White Bear is listed as their leader (Chief). White Bear was a hereditary Chief and during World War I he secured recruits of boys to serve the U.S. He sent his two adopted sons, August and John Brought Plenty to serve in the military. At this time American Indians were not citizens of the U.S. and had no requirement to serve, except for their own U.S. patriotism. The Frosted family also adopted Mary Brought Plenty into their family. (Photo taken by Frank Fiske, c. 1901, postcard courtesy of Donovin Sprague.)

12

KICKS IRON "IRON STAR" (HUNKPAPA).
Roberta Yellow of McLaughlin, S.D. is on
record stating this photo was of Moses Bird
Horse, her grandfather. I have seen photos
of both Kicks Iron and Moses Bird Horse
and the two have a definite resemblance.
(Photo taken by Frank Fiske, c. 1905,
postcard courtesy of Donovin Sprague.)

YELLOW HORSE (YANKTONAI). Yellow
Horse was born near Standing Rock
in 1853. When he was 15 he killed
a Crow Indian in battle. He later led
other successful horse raids into Crow
territory. His medicine was a bird
skin in a yellow cloth. Yellow Horse
married at age 19. Edward Curtis
photographed Yellow Horse and Gray
Bear wearing the same regalia, possibly
loaned by Curtis for the photos. Gray
Bear was also a Yanktonai. (Photo
taken by Edward S. Curtis, 1908,
courtesy of Donovin Sprague.)

ITATEWIN "WOMAN OF THE WINDS" (HUNKPAPA). Itatewin married Charles M. McCarty, a trader, in 1870. She was a cousin of Chief Grasping Eagle. Her first husband was killed by the Crow Indians in battle and her second husband was a white soldier who died at Fort Abercrombie. Charles McCarty came with his parents from Ireland in 1840 and settled south of St. Paul. He served in the Civil War and later arrived in Virginia City, Montana Territory, where he struck gold. He then went to Dakota Territory at Yankton and then north to Standing Rock, where he set up a trading post in 1869 and met Itatewin. A daughter of Itatewin was Mrs. Josephine McCarty Waggoner, a well-known Lakota author, writer, and historian. (Undated photo courtesy of Chester Fuhrman.)

IRON HAWK (HUNKPAPA). This photo was taken in 1900. (Courtesy of South Dakota State Archives).

LITTLE EAGLE (HUNKPAPA). Little Eagle became an Indian policeman at the agency. (Photo taken by Egan, *c.* 1880–1890, courtesy of Denver Public Library.)

RUNNING ANTELOPE "HETON CIKALA INYANKA" (HUNKPAPA). Running Antelope became a head chief (Itancan) in 1851 and was an eloquent speaker for the tribe. His band chose the Little Eagle, S.D. area as their permanent settlement in 1883. Their original camp was where the community hall and gymnasium were later built. The village name became Little Eagle after 1890. In the 1950s, local artist Ambrose Shields painted murals in the gymnasium of the Little Eagle School. The present Little Eagle Day School opened for the 1984–1985 school year with a large area dedicated to veterans of the wars in the entrance driveway. (Photo taken by D.F. Barry, courtesy of Donovin Sprague.)

LOON (STANDING ROCK). Cyril Loon and his wife Elizabeth (Bear Shield) were at Standing Rock by the year of 1889. (Photo taken around 1905–1910 by Frank Fiske, postcard courtesy of Donovin Sprague.)

MRS. CHASING BEAR (STANDING ROCK). (Undated photo taken by Frank Fiske, postcard courtesy of Donovin Sprague.)

LONG SOLDIER "AKICITA HANSKA"
(HUNKPAPA). Long Soldier was a well
known chief at Standing Rock Agency and
represented his band at the signing of the
1868 Treaty of Fort Laramie. In this photo
he holds his pipe and has a nice looking
hat. (Photo taken by O.S. Goff, c. 1874,
postcard courtesy of Donovin Sprague.)

GOOD EAGLE "WANBLI
WASTE" (STANDING ROCK).
This photo was taken during the
Trans-Mississippi Exposition in
Omaha, Nebraska. Records list
the Good Eagle family as Louis
"Wanbli Waste'" and his wife
Yellow Eyes "Istaziwin" with
children Mary, Joseph, Remains
Waihaktawin, and Akanyankakte
Kills Mounted. Louis was born in
1848 and Yellow Eyes in 1853.
This photo may be of another
Good Eagle, based on birth
records of the above family, and
the date of the photo. (Photo
taken by F.A Rinehart, 1898,
courtesy of Donovin Sprague.)

17

CRAZY BEAR "MATO WITKO" (HUNKPAPA). The Crazy Bear name appears in the Standing Rock census of July 1885 with six family members. (Undated photo, courtesy of the Smithsonian Institute.)

CHIEF GALL "PIZI" (HUNKPAPA). Gall was born in Dakota Territory near the Moreau or Grand River about 1840. His mother named him "Matohinshda," which translated to Bear Shedding His Hair. He was later known as Pizi and is well known for his participation at the Battle of the Little Bighorn where he led warriors on attacks of both Major Reno and Custer. At the Little Bighorn Battle Gall lost two wives and three of their children. He stated, "this made my heart bad, I then fought with the hatchet." Middle Cokatnajin is listed as the wife of Gall, born in 1835. He also participated in the Fetterman and Fort Buford Battles in 1866. Gall was a large man, easily over six feet tall. (Photo taken by D.F. Barry, 1881, postcard courtesy of Donovin Sprague.)

SITTING BULL (HUNKPAPA). The famed Itancan and Wicasa Wakan is shown here in an original one cent stamp postcard, # 231 published by E.C. Kropp, Milwaukee. This spiritual leader guided the Hunkpapa for nearly 40 years. Sitting Bull predicted a victory just prior to the Battle of the Little Bighorn when he had a vision in which soldiers were described as falling into camp upside down. He said this meant there would be a great Lakota victory over the soldiers. Custer's soldiers were based just north of present Standing Rock Reservation at Fort Abraham Lincoln. Custer and his troops had arrived at this fort in 1873 and would bring his wife and family members to live at the fort. The vision quest site of Sitting Bull is in eastern Montana, en route to the Little Bighorn. (Undated postcard courtesy of Donovin Sprague.)

SITTING BULL. SIOUX.

JOSEPHINE McCARTY WAGGONER (HUNKPAPA). Josephine was a well-known Lakota author and historian. She was born in October 1872 near the old Grand River Agency in Dakota Territory before Standing Rock was established. Along with her parents, Charles McCarty and Itatewin, she moved to Bismarck, N.D. where her father was the first sheriff of Burleigh County. Charles and his deputy drowned in the frozen Missouri trailing a murderer in 1874–1875. Itatewin and her two daughters then returned to Standing Rock. Josephine attended the Hampton Institute from 1881 to 1888. Returning home, she served as a Lakota language interpreter. While working at Mission Flats, one mile from Fort Yates, she met John Franklin Waggoner of E Company. They married and had four children. At Mission Flats there was a hospital where rations were issued, and there, Josephine interpreted religious services. Sitting Bull, Charging Thunder, and other chiefs attended these services. (Undated photograph courtesy of Chester Fuhrman.)

RAIN IN THE FACE "ITOMAGAJU" (HUNKPAPA). This Chief (Itancan) was well known for his leadership in the Bozeman Trail conflicts including the Fetterman Fight at Fort Phil Kearny on December 21, 1866 and the Battle of the Little Bighorn on June 25, 1876 where some people accused him of cutting out and eating Tom Custer's heart. In an interview shortly before his death, Rain In The Face said that this was not true and was a lie made up by others. At the Battle of the Little Bighorn, Rain In The Face said he fought on the south end against Reno and his soldiers. The Bozeman Trail conflicts in Wyoming and Montana are also referred to as Red Cloud's War, but the northern Lakota bands at Standing Rock and Cheyenne River, including Chief Crazy Horse, did not follow under the Oglala leadership of Red Cloud. They had their own leaders and Rain In The Face was one of them. He is pictured here with a grand warrior society headdress. (Photo taken by D.F. Barry, c. 1885, postcard courtesy of Donovin Sprague.)

SWIFT DOG (STANDING ROCK). This photo was taken at the Omaha Indian Exposition. (Photograph taken in 1898 by F.A. Rinehart, courtesy of the Smithsonian Institute.)

ONE BULL "TATANKA WANJILA" (HUNKPAPA). One Bull was born in 1853 and was a nephew of Sitting Bull. He wore his uncle's shield during the Battle of the Little Bighorn and lived in exile in Canada following the great battle. He stood next to Sitting Bull during their 1881 Fort Buford surrender. One Bull was later known as Henry Oscar One Bull. (Photo by Bailey, Dix, and Mead, Fort Randall, Dakota Territory, 1882, postcard courtesy of Donovin Sprague.)

BEAR'S RIB (HUNKPAPA). This Chief of the Hunkpapa was photographed by Alexander Gardner, Washington, D.C. Bear's Rib was later named Henry James Bear Ribs and his wife was Sarah Pretty Woman. His original name translated to Bear(s) Cuts (Back) Body. Henry was a Chief (Itancan) of a large band of the Grand River Society known as the Sleepy Kettle. This cap identifies him from that warrior society of those living by the Grand River. Some of the tassles on this cap hang to the ground. Bear's Rib signed the 1868 Treaty of Fort Laramie and he lived until 1892. Henry's father was Bear Ribs who signed the 1856 Treaty at Fort Pierre, Dakota Territory; he died in 1862. Henry's son was John Bear Ribs. John's son was killed at the Wounded Knee Massacre in 1890 when they went south to Cheyenne River and Pine Ridge. This son was known as Bear Cuts Body and was 29 years old at that time. His wife's name was Back Of The Head. Today, Terry Bear Ribs is the Great Great Great Grandson of Henry. He provided valuable historical information on Bear's Rib to the author. (Photo taken in 1872, postcard courtesy of Donovin Sprague.)

GALL "PIZI" (HUNKPAPA). This is an early photo of Gall possibly taken on a windy day (lila tate)! This was actually taken in a studio. In 1876 Gall went to Canada and in 1881 he returned to the U.S. to surrender with about 300 followers who were relocated to Standing Rock. He was appointed a boss farmer at the agency in 1885 and joined the Episcopal Church. He appeared briefly in Wild West Shows and became the Judge of the Court of Indian Offenses at Standing Rock. He did not participate in the Ghost Dance movement. (Undated photograph courtesy of Junior Rousseau.)

GOOSE "MAGA" (YANKTONAI). The Goose tiwahe (family) is listed on the Census of Standing Rock Agency of October 1876 as Upper Yantonais band. Goose is also listed as one of the Chiefs of this group. Records of the War Department show Goose enlisted with the U.S. Army as a Scout in 1876 and served almost continuously until 1882. He enlisted again in 1891 at Fort Yates and was honorably discharged in 1893. Goose died in September, 1915. (Photo taken by D.F. Barry, courtesy of the Smithsonian Institute.)

MRS. JACK TREETOP (STANDING ROCK). Early records about the Treetop family indicate that Jack Treetop had a wife named Edith Slowbull and a child of theirs named Agnes Katherine Treetop was born at Fort Yates in 1900 and lived until 1984. Edith Slowbull was born in 1881 at Fort Yates. Her father was Slowbull, born in 1841 and her mother was Walk Slomaniwin, who was born in 1846. A brother of Edith's was Chase Alone, who was born in 1878 at Fort Yates. Edith Slowbull was also married to John Theophylus Treetop in 1898. John Treetop was born in 1876. Later Treetop names from Cannonball, N.D. are Michael, born in 1910 and Julia, born in 1923. (Photo taken by Frank Fiske, *c.* 1908, postcard courtesy of Donovin Sprague and SHSND.)

COTTONWOOD (YANKTONAI). The photographer D.F. Barry recorded that Cottonwood possessed a rifle that he picked up at the Battle of the Little Bighorn. Jerome Cottonwood was at Fort Yates as early as 1870. Cottonwood is listed in the early Standing Rock Census of 1876 as head of the Cottonwood tiospaye (extended family) and tiwahe (family) among the Lower Yanktonais. He would be considered a Chief at the agency. (Photo taken by D.F. Barry, courtesy of the Smithsonian Institute.)

ONE BULL (HUNKPAPA/MINNICOUJOU). One Bull is the nephew of Sitting Bull and on this photo it reads that he is cooking beef. The photo reads "McIntosh, S.D. by H.W." Rocks could be heated at the fireplace and then placed into the hanging container that was often the stomach of a buffalo. Water and meat placed in the container would then be cooked in a boiling process. (Undated photograph courtesy of Jack Bickel.)

CHIEF GRAY EAGLE AND FAMILY (HUNKPAPA). This is an old stereoview card, # 436. Chief Gray Eagle is seated on the right and his wife and child are standing at the tipi entrance. His son is standing at the left and the card says his name is Tomahawk. (Photo by T.W. Ingersoll, 1899, stereoview card courtesy of Donovin Sprague.)

LOUISE STANDING SOLDIER
(HUNKPAPA). Louise was
born in 1852 and married
Akicita Najin (Standing
Soldier). He became known
as David Standing Soldier and
a child of theirs was born in
1895 at Fort Yates by the name
of Kuwa Standing Soldier.
David Standing Soldier was
born in 1852. Unclassified
data researched by the author
pertaining to Louise is as
follows: "Charles and Rachel
(Standing Soldier) Dunn –
George and Louise." (Undated
photograph courtesy of Melvin
White Eagle and SHSND.)

CHIEF TWO BEAR (YANKTONAI). The
author has another picture from this
photo session which has Two Bear's
son and daughter standing beside him.
(Undated photo taken by D.F. Barry,
courtesy of the Smithsonian Institute.)

25

ROBERT P. HIGH EAGLE "WANBLI
WANKATUYA" (HUNKPAPA). Robert was
a graduate of the Hampton Institute in
Virginia, and of the business department
of Carnegie College. He also attended the
University of Chicago. He collaborated with
Frances Densmore on her study of music
and culture for the Smithsonian's Bureau
of American Ethnology on Standing Rock
Reservation, and at Sisseton Wahpeton
Reservation in South Dakota during the years
1911–1914. The studies were published in the
book *Teton Music & Culture* and Robert served
as a translator and cultural mediator. He was a
Catholic and built three churches in the Little
Eagle area. Robert married a woman from
Sisseton. Annie Loneman was a half sister of
Robert's and Ray Higheagle of Rapid City,
S.D. is his grandson. Ray has been involved
in developing many programs beneficial
to American Indians. The High Eagle/
Higheagle family is not related to the High
Eagle pictured with the 1948 Little Bighorn
survivors, who was from Pine Ridge. (Undated
photograph courtesy of Donovin Sprague.)

GOOD HORSE AND FAMILY (LAKOTA). Good
Horse led his warriors in the Battle of the Rosebud
against General Crook and at the Battle of the
Little Bighorn. Information on the photo states
Good Horse was a cousin of Crazy Horse. There
is no proven photo ever taken of Crazy Horse but
he is remembered in this book and is a part of the
history of the bands who reside at Standing Rock.
Crazy Horse spent as much time in the northern
Lakota lands allied with the Hunkpapa as he did in
the southern Lakota lands. He had an alliance with
Sitting Bull and many other leaders. Although Crazy
Horse is associated in books as an Oglala Lakota
he was a Minnicoujou and spent his life with his
Minnicoujou relatives High Back Bone (Hump I),
Hump (II, son of High Back Bone), and Touch The
Cloud. His mother was Rattling Blanket Woman,
a Minnicoujou from the Lone Horn (One Horn)
family. His father Waglula (Worm) also traces to
the Minnicoujou, with some debating that Worm
was also Oglala and Sicangu. Touch The Cloud
and Si Tanka (Big Foot) were two of Lone Horn's
well known sons. The northern Lakota were the
last holdouts in the war against the U.S. (Undated
photograph courtesy of the Smithsonian Institute.)

TWO SHIELDS (STANDING ROCK).
Two Shields provided information to
Frances Densmore in her studies of
music and culture at Standing Rock. He
related a dream into song about wolves,
and the song learned from the wolf was
the beginning of wolf songs (war songs).
From this the people began the custom
of carrying a wolf skin medicine bag.
(Undated photo taken by Frank Fiske,
courtesy of the Smithsonian Institute.)

**BUFFALO BOY FAMILY "TATANKA
HOKSILA TIWAHE" (STANDING ROCK).**
Herbert Buffalo Boy was listed at Standing
Rock by 1915. Pictured here, from left
to right, are: (back row) Mrs. Conrad
Buffalo Boy and Mrs. Herbert Buffalo
Boy (The wife of Herbert was the former
Josephine White Cloud); (seated in
the middle) Conrad Buffalo Boy (with
headdress) and Herbert Buffalo Boy;
(front row) Agatha Buffalo Boy and
Laura Buffalo Boy. (Undated photograph
courtesy of Melvin White Eagle/SHSND.)

LITTLE SOLDIER (YANKTONAI). Chief Little Soldier was listed as a headman in the Standing Rock census of 1876 under the Lower Yanktonais but would also be Hunkpapa. In the Selfridge, N.D. community history, the Little Soldier family is listed among the earliest families living in the area. Before 1902 Little Soldier moved to where the Lund farm is located. The mother of Little Soldier was Four Robes. (Undated photograph courtesy of the Smithsonian Institute.)

MAN ON THE HILL AND HIS WIFE (NORTHERN LAKOTA). This couple belonged to one of the Cheyenne River or Standing Rock Lakota bands, probably mixed. The wife's name was not recorded at the time. They have trade blankets, dentalium shell necklaces with abalone shell, calico shirt and dress, a pipe/tomahawk, shoulder bag, and a braided lariat rope. This would be another family surrendering from their northern U.S./Canada homeland. (Photo taken by L.A. Huffman at Fort Keogh, Montana Territory, 1880, courtesy of Coffrin's Old West Gallery, Bozeman, Montana.)

JOHN SITTING BULL (HUNKPAPA). John Sitting Bull was also known as Refuses Them. He was a movie star, and traveled with the Wild West Shows despite having a hearing impairment. His half brother was Henry Little Soldier and Henry's mother was Four Robes. John's mother was Seen By Her Nation. Their father was Bear Louse, not Sitting Bull. John's sister was named Killed, and John's grandmother on his fathers side was called Talks A Lot. Talks A Lot was not a Grey Eagle. (Photo taken c. 1950s, courtesy of Ernie LaPointe and Ethel Bates.)

JOHN GRASS "PEZI" (SIHA SAPA). John Grass was very active in the Bozeman Trail wars as a leader (Itancan). Later he became known to the U.S. army as a great orator and diplomat. He traveled to Washington, DC with Standing Rock and Cheyenne River delegations. For 30 years he was the leading judge of the Court of Indian Offenses at Standing Rock. John was born in 1869 and records show he had marriages to Annie Alkire in 1896, to Isabella in 1890, and Amanda in 1881. His father was also named John "Matowatakpe" Grass (Pezi) who was born in 1846. The father was also known as Used As A Shield "Wahacankayapi" and was a noted warrior against other tribes, but was always friendly toward white people. The mother of Annie Alkire was Mary "Tacanonpa" Alkire. (Portrait by H.H. Cross, photograph courtesy of Donovin Sprague.)

SPOTTED BEAR (HUNKPAPA).
Many of the northern Lakota would surrender and be placed at Fort Keogh, including Standing Rock and Cheyenne River Lakota bands. In April 1881 there were 156 more Hunkpapa who arrived at Fort Keogh, mostly from Canada, to surrender. These people would later be transferred to Dakota Territory. The U.S. military split up Lakota leadership and separated the main Itancan (Chiefs/leaders) at different forts to exercise total control and confinement of the Lakota. (Photo taken by L.A. Huffman at Fort Keogh, Montana Territory, 1878, courtesy of Frank Ross at Coffrin's Old West Gallery, Bozeman, MT.)

CHIEF TWO BEAR "MAHTO NUPA" (YANKTONAI). This photo is undated. The son of Chief Two Bear is pictured on page 25. A granddaughter of Chief Two Bear was Josephine Gates Kelly, and Josephine's daughter Susan Kelly Power of Chicago is the Two Bear family historian today. (Courtesy of Susan Kelly Power.)

BULL HEAD (YANKTONAI). Bull Head became a Lieutenant with the Indian police at Standing Rock. Bull Head was in charge of Indian police sent by Agent James McLaughlin to arrest Sitting Bull on December 15, 1890. Bull Head and Sitting Bull both were shot and killed when a fight broke out during the attempted arrest. The Indian police were put in a very difficult and volatile situation. In this photo of Bull Head he holds a Pipe of which both the bowl and stem is made of red pipestone from the Minnesota quarry. The Bull Head family is listed among the Upper Yantonais in the 1876 Standing Rock Census and included as a headman family. Earl Bull Head is a great great great grandson of Bull Head and stated that Bull Head's first name became either Henry or Frank. (Photo taken by D.F. Barry, 1880s, courtesy of the Smithsonian Institute.)

CHIEF GALL "PIZI" (HUNKPAPA). This Itancan (leader) fled to Canada following his participation at the Battle of the Little Bighorn. He surrendered in 1881 and returned to Dakota Territory where he became a leader for peace. From 1889 until his death in 1894 he served as a Judge of the Court of Indian Offenses at Standing Rock Agency. Gall was laid to rest at St. Elizabeth's Mission near Wakpala, S.D. (Photograph courtesy of Denver Public Library.)

31

JOHN GRASS "PEZI" (SIHA SAPA).
John Grass was earlier known as Charging Bear "Mato Wathape". The attire he is wearing here has an interesting story. The shirt became famous when Red Cloud (Oglala) posed with it and it was identified as his. However, the shirt really belonged to Chief Smoke "Shota" (Oglala/Sicangu/Siha Sapa). Smithsonian records show the shirt was a gift from Smoke to William O. Collins prior to 1864. Red Cloud was Smoke's uncle. The shirt fit Smoke's 250 pound frame and has a Cheyenne design and color. It was brought out for photo sessions at the Smithsonian. There are photos of Smoke, Red Cloud, Squint Eye (Cheyenne), and John Grass all wearing Smoke's regalia. John Grass is the last known person to be photographed with it in this 1912 photo. He is wearing an American cotton shirt under the buckskin shirt. (The collar is visible around his neck.) Even Smoke's human remains were at the Smithsonian until they were repatriated home in 1994. (Photograph taken by Delancey Gill in Washington, D.C., 1912, courtesy of the Smithsonian Institute.)

RED BIRD "ZINTKALA LUTA" (STANDING ROCK). Early records of the Red Bird family from Standing Rock list Martin Red Bird as the head of the household (born in 1872), his wife Nora Red Bird (born in 1876), and a son named Joseph Red Bird (born in 1895). The Red Bird family is also at Cheyenne River Reservation. (Undated photograph courtesy of the Smithsonian Institute.)

LAKOTA WINYAN AND CINKSI (LAKOTA WOMEN AND SON). These unidentified women and child are in camp and preparing dinner. Iron trade kettles sometimes replaced cooking that was done in the dried stomach of a buffalo. Antlers are balancing the kettle in this photo, keeping it raised above the fire. The woman on the right has a dried hide which contains meal she is breaking up. A dried and painted parfleche bag lays behind the kettle. This bag could hold stored food. Animal fat could also be melted and dried onto the edges of the parfleche bag to make the bag air tight and preserve the food from spoiling. (Photo by Heyn, 1899, postcard courtesy of Donovin Sprague.)

RUNNING ANTELOPE, "HETON CIKALA INYANKA" (HUNKPAPA). This photo combined the 1872 photo of Running Antelope taken by Alexander Gardner and a photo of a headdress taken by Thomas W. Smillie in 1899. This became the United States five dollar certificate in 1899. (Photograph courtesy of Donovin Sprague.)

JAW "CEHUPA" (STANDING ROCK).
Jaw (Cehupa) lived just west of
Bullhead, S.D. He was a historian
and artist and recorded valuable
cultural history of the tribe and
community. He recorded history
onto ledger drawings, and was a
good friend of Frank Shooter from
Bullhead. There were two different
men by the name of Jaw. Records
obtained on one of these men
known as Jaw indicate he was born
in 1853 at Fort Yates and married
Tamila Kokipapa (Afraid of Her
Knife/Fear Her Knife) in 1872. His
wife was born in the year of 1851.
These records may be from an older
Jaw. (Undated photograph courtesy
of the Smithsonian Institute.)

**RED FISH "HOGAN LUTA" AND
DAUGHTERS (SANTEE/YANKTONAI).**
Red Fish was a Chief (Itancan)
and an important member of the
councils of the tribe. He was present
at a Dakota Territory hearing in
which a select committee of the
Senate from Washington, DC was
sent to investigate the condition of
the Indian tribes of Montana and
Dakota. Spokesmen were John Grass
(Siha Sapa), Running Antelope
and Sitting Bull (both Hunkpapa).
Agent McLaughlin said the Upper and
Lower Yanktonais at Standing Rock
had no spokesmen because they had
no concerns about policy, although
Red Fish was part Yanktonai. (Photo
taken by Frank Fiske, c. 1900-1904,
postcard courtesy of Donovin Sprague.)

BLACK BEAR "MATO SAPA" (STANDING ROCK). Black Bear families were listed as Lower Yanktonai in the Standing Rock census of July 1885. (Undated photo taken by Frank Fiske, postcard courtesy of Donovin Sprague.)

HATTIE LAWRENCE "CANKU LAWIN" (STANDING ROCK). Hattie Lawrence attended Carlisle Indian School and assisted Frances Densmore as an interpreter at McLaughlin, S.D. She also contributed a song for Densmore's book, which was an honor song for Hattie's cousin Kimimila Ska (White Butterfly) who was killed by the Crow Indians. Hattie was ten years old when this happened and remembered her aunt singing the song when the war party returned with the news of his death. She said her aunt lost another son and a song was also recorded for him. (Undated photograph courtesy of the Smithsonian Institute.)

ONE BULL (ON LEFT) AND WHITE BULL (MINNICOUJOU/HUNKPAPA). White Bull was a nephew of Sitting Bull and a brother of One Bull. They both have ties to Standing Rock and Cheyenne River and White Bull resided at both locations during his lifetime. The brothers were the sons of Chief Makes Room "Kiukanpi" (Minnicoujou) and Sitting Bull's sister Good Feather "Wiyaka Wastewin" (Hunkpapa). (Photo from Huettner Collection, undated, courtesy of Klein Museum, Mobridge, S.D.)

BUFFALO BOY "TATANKA HOKSILA" (SANTEE/YANKTONAI). Buffalo Boy received his name from a dream in which he saw the buffalo. A later generation, Herbert Buffalo Boy, was cited for valuable service under General Patton in World War II. He drove a Jeep for General Patton and may have been a Drill Sergeant. The postcard was produced by Conlin's Gallery of Miles City, MT. (Undated photo taken by L.A. Huffman, postcard courtesy of Donovin Sprague.)

No Heart "Cante Wanica" (Yanktonai).
No Heart was a well known medicine man of the tribe and an artist. His artwork included drawings of tribal ceremonies. Frances Densmore included No Heart's drawings in her study of music, dance, culture, and ceremony at Standing Rock. (Undated photograph courtesy of the Smithsonian Institute.)

Rain in the Face "Itomagaju" (Hunkpapa). Rain In The Face was once held captive at Fort Lincoln but escaped and later participated in the Battle of the Little Bighorn. Rain In The Face described one of his early successful fights which was a daring attack at Fort Totten. He was born in 1835 and journeyed to the spirit world on September 14, 1905 at the age of 70. (Photo taken by Fiske, *c.* 1902, postcard courtesy of Donovin Sprague.)

RED TOMAHAWK (HUNKPAPA).
Red Tomahawk was part of the Indian police who exchanged gunfire with Sitting Bull and his followers during the attempted arrest of the leader. (Photo taken by Frank Fiske, c. 1890-1910, photograph courtesy of Denver Public Library.)

CHIEF WHITE BULL (MINNICOUJOU).
White Bull was the brother of One Bull and both were nephews of Sitting Bull. White Bull moved to Cheyenne River and is affiliated with both Minnicoujou and Hunkpapa. (Photo taken c. 1870–1890, courtesy of the Smithsonian Institute.)

SITTING BULL "TATANKA IYOTAKE" (HUNKPAPA). Sitting Bull is wearing two feathers and the one on the left that is leaning was painted red, representing wounds he had received. (Undated photo from Huettner Collection, courtesy of Klein Museum, Mobridge, S.D.)

RED FOX (STANDING ROCK). Red Fox is shown here with sunglasses. The Red Fox name is listed in the 1876 census under the Itancan (leader) Red Bull. Red Fox was sometimes known as "Rattles" and was in battle against the Crow with Sitting Bull, Loud Bear, Spotted Weasel, Thrown On Ground, Scatters Them, Running Hawk, and Wooden Gun. Red Fox was later in another fight against the Crow when Sitting Bull's father Jumping Bull was killed at Rainy Butte in Slope County, ND. Many other well known Hunkpapa were also present. Red Fox participated in the Battle of the Rosebud just prior to the Battle of the Little Bighorn in June, 1876 when General Crook and his forces were defeated. Other Hunkpapa's at the Rosebud were: Sitting Bull, One Bull, White Bull (Minnicoujou/Hunkpapa), Old Bull, Gray Eagle, Bear Soldier, Black Bear, Flying Bye, Little Moon, and Red Bird. (Photo taken by Frank Fiske, c.1910, postcard courtesy of Donovin Sprague.)

BUFFALO BILL'S WILD WEST SHOW IN OMAHA. This is the grand entry of the Wild West Show. The show premiered in Columbus, Nebraska and continued for 31 years until 1913. Many people from Standing Rock were participants in the show throughout the world, including Sitting Bull. (Photo taken by J.E. Stimson, 1907, postcard courtesy of Donovin Sprague.)

STANDING ROCK TIPIS. This undated photo was taken at Standing Rock Reservation. The tipis were very unique in their construction and design. These tipis were made of canvas but the old ones were made from buffalo robes sewn together. The man often painted his exploits on the tipi, but it was owned by the woman of the household. Studies on the tipi were completed by Reginald and Gladys Laubin, who visited Standing Rock and interviewed people. Their book *The Indian Tipi: Its History, Construction, and Use* contained much useful information. They also did books on archery, dances, and ceremony. Resource people they cited included Francis Zahn (Flying Cloud), Chief One Bull, Little Soldier, Philip Returns From Scout, and Kills Pretty Enemy. (Photograph courtesy of Sioux County History book staff.)

HUNKPAPA LAKOTA LODGES. The tipi lodges are made of buffalo hide and the man at left may be gathering wooden tipi poles. At the center of the camp meat is hanging to be dried. (Photo taken by L.A. Huffman near Fort Keogh, Montana Territory, 1878, courtesy of Coffrin's Old West Gallery, Bozeman, MT.)

CHIEF THUNDER HAWK "CETAN WAKIYAN" (STANDING ROCK). Early family names of Thunder Hawk's at Standing Rock were Thunder Hawk (born about 1864) and his wife Elizabeth Eagle Staff (born about 1868). A son of theirs was John Charles Thunder Hawk, who was born in 1890 and married Katherine "Kate" Streaked Eye. The Thunderhawk pictured here once saved the life of Father DeSmet. The town of Thunder Hawk, S.D is named for him or his family. The author knows the Thunder Hawk family at Pine Ridge Indian Reservation and some have relatives and probable origins to the Hunkpapa. (Undated photograph courtesy of *Teton Times*.)

JOE NO HEART "CANTE WANICA" (STANDING ROCK). Joseph "Cante Wanica" No Heart was born in 1843 and married Blue Day "Anpetuto" in 1873. Blue Day "Anpetuto" was born in 1847. Joseph is shown here as an Indian policeman. (Photo taken by Frank Fiske, *c.* 1906-1910, postcard courtesy of Donovin Sprague.)

GRAY HAWK (HUNKPAPA). Gray Hawk's golden eagle headdress is trimmed with hair and ribbons and has a beaded headband adorned with prairie chicken feathers. Clam shell ornaments decorate the fur throat piece. The breast plate is of milk glass tube beads spaced with elk hide strips and decorated with trade mirrors. He holds a bow and arrows with a quiver. (Undated photo taken by Fiske, postcard courtesy of Donovin Sprague.)

Paul Brave Family "Ohitika Tiwahe" (Standing Rock).
Paul "Ohitika" Brave is pictured here with his wife Genevieve Brave and their daughter. Paul was born in 1867 and Genevieve was born in 1868. The photographer did not identify Paul's wife and daughter in this photo. They also had a son named Peter Brave who was born in 1895. (Undated photo taken by Frank Fiske, postcard courtesy of Donovin Sprague.)

Unidentified Itancan (Leader).
This man is pictured with a studio background holding a Canunpa (Pipe) and pipe bag. (Undated photo from Oscar Huettner Collection, courtesy of Klein Museum, Mobridge, S.D)

MRS. PHILIP "TOKAOLE" BULLHEAD AND BROWNTRACK (STANDING ROCK). Henrietta Bullhead married Philip "Tokaole" Bullhead and they also had a son named Philip Bullhead who was born in 1895. Philip, Sr. was born in 1857 and this photo is likely Henrietta since the photo was probably taken in the time period after the birth of Philip, Jr. (Undated photo likely by Frank Fiske, courtesy of Donovin Sprague and SHSND.)

ANNIE GATES ARCHAMBAULT (YANKTONAI). Annie Gates was born on April 19, 1883 and was the daughter of Frank Gates and his wife Nellie Two Bear-Gates. Annie married Louis Archambault on October 19, 1902 at St. Peters Church at Standing Rock. Louis served as a guide and interpreter when Fort Yates was being considered as a site for the Standing Rock Agency headquarters. Annie is the granddaughter of Chief Two Bear, and her sister Mary Gates married Joseph Archambault, a half brother to Louis "Louie" Archambault. Annie Gates Archambault died in 1931 at age 48. (Undated photo likely by Fiske, courtesy of Donovin Sprague and SHSND.)

Two

OWAKPAMNI TOKAHE
EHANNI
(EARLY AGENCY ERA)

BULLHEAD, S.D. This is a July 4th celebration at the community of Bullhead, probably in the early 1900s. (Photograph courtesy of Jack Bickel.)

MR. AND MRS. FLYING BYE
(HUNKPAPA). There are two families of
Flying Bye and Flying By at Standing
Rock who are not related. This photo
could be the George Flying Bye family.
Wilbur Flying By of Sitting Bull
College is from another family and
said the spelling was changed at the
agency from Flying By to Flying Bye.
Two earlier names of famous wicasa
wakan (medicine men) from Wilbur's
family are Dreamer of the Sun/Sun
Dreamer and Chief Leon Kills Pretty
Enemy. They were respected medicine
men and leaders of the people. They
used their knowledge of the religion
and herbs for healing people. In 1887 a
Catholic School was established at the
Flying By Settlement about five miles
downstream from Running Antelope
Settlement. Running Antelope
Settlement was renamed Little Eagle,
S.D. (Undated photo by Frank Fiske,
courtesy of SHSND Fiske 2190.)

HAIRY CHIN (HUNKPAPA). Chief Hairy Chin
and his wife Josephine Two Bear-Hairy Chin
were among the early residents at Fort Yates in
1870. They also lived at Shields, ND, in the
Porcupine District. On July 4, 1889 noted chiefs
at Standing Rock participated in a parade at
Bismarck, ND. They included Gall, Rain In The
Face, John Grass, Goose, Mad Bear, Crow Eagle,
Flying Bye, Sitting Bull, Two Bear, Long Dog,
Fire Cloud, Long Feather, Low Dog, Crow King,
High Bear, Gray Eagle, Crow, Fool Thunder, Red
Horse, and Red Fish. Agent McLaughlin was
in command and dressed Hairy Chin as Uncle
Sam to lead the parade. Two days later after the
return to Standing Rock, Hairy Chin died. He
was a brother to Chief Long Dog. The people
believed his dress had something to do with his
mysterious death, and no one would ever appear
again as Uncle Sam. Emory Dean Keoke is a great
great grandson of Hairy Chin and is the author
of *Native American Contributions To The World*.
There is another Hairy Chin family at Standing
Rock, but they are not blood line relatives to
Chief Hairy Chin. (Photo taken by D.F. Barry,
1889, courtesy of the Smithsonian Institute.)

CHIEF GALL AND WILLIAM HAWK (HUNKPAPA). Gall is posed with a Christian cross in the studio with his nephew William Hawk. He later took the name John at the agency. The people chose or were assigned first names that were often names from the Bible. (Photo taken by D.F. Barry, 1880s, courtesy of Denver Public Library.)

SAMUEL GAYTON FAMILY (STANDING ROCK). Sam Gayton married Margaret Mulhern, and their children were Jane, Rose, Louise, Annie, Alfred, William, Henry, John, Arthur, Alfred, Ruby, Harry, Minnie, and Evelyn. (The first Alfred listed here died at the age of 14 months). Sam was at Standing Rock as early as 1892 and is getting his family started here. (Undated photograph courtesy of Melvin White Eagle/SHSND.)

BEEF ISSUE DAY AT STANDING ROCK. This rare stereoview picture shows tribal members obtaining their monthly issue of food provided by the U.S. Government. A man and woman are butchering the beef and the women in the background are loading the prepared meat into wagons. The people were once self sufficient in obtaining buffalo and other food but were now reliant upon the U.S. to provide them with food. Much of the beef came from Texas; longhorn cattle were driven north by white contractors. The early reports were that the Plains Indians did not like the taste of beef as they preferred the lean buffalo meat, which was now depleted. (Photo # 430 taken c. 1899, stereoview card courtesy of Donovin Sprague.)

SIOUX INDIANS AT MANDAN, ND. This is an old postcard of an unidentified group in traditional dress at Mandan, ND. Mandan is about 50 miles north of Standing Rock Reservation with a population of just over 15,500 and is just across the Missouri River from Bismarck, ND. (Undated photo taken by Lutz, postcard courtesy of Donovin Sprague.)

LOUIS AND MONICA AGARD WITH DAUGHTER MARY ROSE AGARD (FRENCH/ STANDING ROCK). Louis Agard was born on Dec. 20, 1864 and was the son of Louis/ Tatelinn Agard, Sr. who came from France, where he was born in 1838. Louis Sr. married Mary Spotted Horse, who was born in Dakota Territory (South Dakota) in 1842. Louis Agard, Jr. married Monica C. Winasteka in 1888. Monica was born in 1868 and was the daughter of Walking Eagle, who was born in Dakota Territory (South Dakota) in 1842. Monica died at the age of 43 in 1911 at Fort Yates, ND. The daughter of Louis and Monica was Mary Rose Agard, who was born July 2, 1890 in Corson County, S.D and lived until the age of 58 when she passed away on March 20, 1959. Either Louis Sr. or Louis Jr. had worked at many forts and posts and during his travels had married a total of 22 winyan (women). This photo is probably of Louis Sr. (Photo could be by Fiske, c.1891, courtesy of Melvin White Eagle.)

LUCILLE VAN SOLEN (STANDING ROCK). Lucille Van Solen was born in 1883 at Fort Yates to Mrs. M.L. Van Solen. They lived at Cannon Ball when it was located north of the Cannon Ball River. Lucille's mother was French and Indian and her sister was Mrs. H.S. Parkins, whose husband had a large ranch. Mrs. Van Solen and daughter Lucille inherited the ranch when both Parkins died. Mrs. Van Solen was a school teacher and the town of Solen, ND is named for her. Lucille and her mother were both buried on a high hill overlooking the Cannon Ball River. (Undated photo likely by Fiske, courtesy of Melvin White Eagle/SHSND.)

JOHN ARCHAMBAULT AND JOHN GATES (STANDING ROCK). Records indicate John Archambault (Sr.?) was born in 1864. John Gates was born in 1892, the son of Frank and Nellie Two Bear-Gates. John's brothers and sisters included Francis, Annie, Mary, Josephine, and Edward. John's father was born in 1852 and his mother was born in 1855. His sister Annie Gates married Louis Archambault. A sister of Nellie Two Bear-Gates was Josephine Two Bear who married Chief Hairy Chin. (Undated postcard courtesy of Donovin Sprague.)

JOSEPHINE PLEETS (HUNKPAPA). Photo
taken by Frank Fiske, undated. Josephine
Zahn married Jesse Pleets. Jesse was employed
for several years with the Bureau of Indian
Affairs at Fort Yates until retirement.
Wilbur "Banny" Pleets is one of their
nephews. Four children of George Pleets all
attended Hampton Institute during the years
1878-1890. George Pleets was the Great
Great Grandfather of Wilbur "Banny" Pleets.
(Undated photo taken by Frank Fiske,
courtesy of Melvin White Eagle/SHSND.)

MR. AND MRS. ALBERT NO HEART "CANTE
WANICA" (STANDING ROCK). The No Heart
family posed here, probably in the studio of
Frank B. Fiske. Albert No Heart was listed
at Standing Rock in 1915. Records show
that Albert was born in 1874 and married
Tamaza Strike The Ree in 1888. They had
three daughters, Stands-Tanyaninajiwin, Good
Will-Tawacinwastewin, Warrior-Zuye, and a
son named George No Heart. They are listed
here in order of their birth. Albert was later
married to Lucy Lean Elk and their children
were Agnes, Albert, Jr. (born in 1918), and
Harry. (Undated photograph courtesy of
Donovin Sprague/SHSND.)

LUKE EAGLEMAN, SR. AND SAMUEL CADOTTE (HUNKPAPA). Samuel Cadotte was the father of Gene Cadotte and Daisy Cadotte LeCompte. Samuel was born in 1881 and his mother was Red Cloud Woman "Mahpiya Luta Win who was born in 1840. Luke Eagleman, Sr. was the grandfather of Charmayne Eagleman, who provided the photo. Luke was born in 1878 and married Amy Shoot The Bear who was born in 1883. They were married at St. Elizabeth's Episcopal Church in Wakpala, S.D in 1903, and had four sons and four daughters. Their son Oliver Eagleman of Wakpala provided assistance to the author. (Undated, photograph courtesy of Charmayne Eagleman.)

LOUISE STRICKER (YANKTONAI). Louise Stricker married Howard Standing Bear, and this photo was submitted by Charmayne Eagleman of Wakpala, S.D. (Undated photograph courtesy of Charmayne Eagleman.)

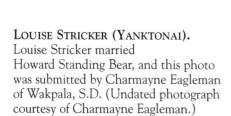

Three

Unci Makoce Etanhan
Skinciyapi na Inakiya
(Struggles for Freedom and
Surrenders from Canada)

Wood Mountain Area, Saskatchewan, Canada. The area of Wood Mountain and Willow Bunch in Saskatchewan is where many Lakota groups fled following the Battle of the Little Bighorn and after the death of Crazy Horse. Most of the people were from the Hunkpapa and Siha Sapa bands but there were also Lakota's of the Minnicoujou, Itazipco, Oohenumpa, and Oglala. This area is remote with few people, and the landscape is not unlike the area of Standing Rock Reservation. Members of the Assiniboine, Dakota, Metis, and French traders were also in this area. Sitting Bull, Gall, Rain In The Face, Black Moon, Black Bull, Hump, Little Knife, Long Dog, The Man Who Crawls, White Eagle, and Four Horns were a few of the leaders who traveled here. The Dakota leaders Standing Buffalo and White Cap were to the north, and the Blackfeet to the west. Sitting Bull befriended Chief Crow Foot of the Blackfeet and named his son after this leader. To the far north in Saskatoon, the author heard accounts of their White Cap Dakota people traveling south to meet Sitting Bull along with some of their people who were allied in warfare with their Lakota relatives against the U.S. (Photo taken in 2003, courtesy of Donovin Sprague.)

CROW KING "KANGI YATAPI"
(HUNKPAPA). Crow King was born
about 1837 and was baptized as a
Catholic in 1883, taking the name
Joachim Crow King. He married
Anna Tokeyahinanpewin and later
died of pneumonia in 1884, leaving
two daughters Mary Crow King and
Emma Crow King. Mary died in 1885
and Emma married Paul Cournoyer.
Chief Crow King led his warriors at
the Battle of the Little Bighorn. This
photo was taken during his surrender
from Canada at Fort Buford, Dakota
Territory, where he was presented
with this soldier's uniform. (Photo
taken by D.F. Barry, 1881, postcard
courtesy of Donovin Sprague.)

FORT BUFORD, ND. Following U.S. and Lakota conflicts such as at Killdeer Mountain near the Little Missouri, General Sully would establish Fort Buford in 1866. Like the forts along the Bozeman Trail, soldiers were usually confined to the fort, with Lakotas everywhere around them. The fort was at the confluence of the Yellowstone River and the Missouri River. Many Lakota bands surrendered here, including Sitting Bull on July 20, 1881. Many of the northern Lakotas made their surrender to Nelson Miles, but Sitting Bull surrendered here to Major David H. Brotherton. At the surrender he gave his son his Model 1866 .44 caliber Winchester rifle to give to Brotherton. In 1946 it was donated to the Smithsonian by an heir. The fort is near Williston, ND and was rebuilt. Earlier, Fort Union was established nearby by John Jacob Astor's American Fur Company in 1829 and in 1832 artist George Catlin spent time at the fort, as well as artist Karl Bodmer. In 1867 Fort Union was sold to the army and the fort was dismantled and the materials were used to build Fort Buford. Today, the Fort Union location is one and a half miles west of Fort Buford. (Photo taken in 2003, photograph courtesy of Donovin Sprague.)

BLACK BULL "TATANKA SAPA" (HUNKPAPA). This telegram was sent on September 30, 1884 from Moose Jaw, Northwest Territory (Saskatchewan, Canada) to notify that Black Bull, who was allied with Sitting Bull, did not return to the U.S. to surrender. Many northern Lakota bands remained in southwest Saskatchewan, southern Alberta, and as far north as Moose Jaw, Saskatchewan. The telegram reads "Coat Of Arms" and is signed "Tatonka Sappa, Right Bearer to Tatonka Yotaka or Sitting Bull in Custer Massacre." The signature of Tatanka Sapa (Black Bull) is a drawing of a black buffalo bull. The author received this telegram from George Halliday of Minnesota, who said it came from his grandfather who worked for the railroads. (Photograph courtesy of George Halliday and Donovin Sprague.)

CHIEF BLACK BULL "TATANKA SAPA" (HUNKPAPA). The Black Bull family also spent time in Canada before surrendering and returning to the U.S. Black Bull was also a scout for the U.S. at Fort Yates, ND. (Photo taken at Crane's Studio, July 13, 1900, courtesy of Denver Public Library.)

DAVID F. BARRY AND RAIN IN THE FACE (HUNKPAPA). The photographer David F. Barry is pictured here in the studio with Rain In The Face holding his rifle. Barry said, "Rain In The Face was the most docile Indian that ever sat before my camera. He was always willing to pose, and had a ready palm for gifts. He was a great convenience to me in keeping down my stock of linen, for he also had a mania for white shirts." Rain In The Face said he was born near the forks of the Cheyenne River and got his name when he won a friendly fight with a Cheyenne boy when he was about ten years old. Rain In The Face won the fight but the Cheyenne boy hit him in the face several times and his face was covered with blood and streaked where his war paint had washed away. Other Lakota boys who watched the action then gave him his name. Frank Fiske married Angela Cournoyer. (Photo taken by D.F. Barry, c.1889, photograph courtesy of the Smithsonian Institute.)

LEFT TO RIGHT: CROW KING (HUNKPAPA), MAJOR DAVID BROTHERTON, GEORGE FLEURY (STANDING), AND LOW DOG (SIHA SAPA). This photo was taken during the surrender at Fort Buford when Crow King and Low Dog returned from Canada and surrendered to Major David Brotherton. Crow King was given a military uniform which he wears here. George Fleury was the French/Indian interpreter for Fort Buford. Low Dog is always listed as an Oglala but is a Siha Sapa. His family went south and Cheyenne River Sioux tribal member Carideo Low Dog of Dupree, S.D is the great grandson of Chief Low Dog. Madeline "Maggie" Low Dog Handboy was a granddaughter of Low Dog and she was probably enrolled as an Oglala since the family has ties to Pine Ridge Reservation also. Maggie married Raymond Handboy, a Minnicoujou, so the family became a mixture of Lakota bands in later generations. The author has interviewed Carideo and Estherlene Low Dog and the Handboy family for a previous book. Crow King and Low Dog were both participants in the Battle of the Little Bighorn. (Photo taken by D.F. Barry, May 1881, photograph courtesy of the Smithsonian Institute.)

SITTING BULL "TATANKA IYOTAKE" (HUNKPAPA).
Following the Lakota/Dakota and Cheyenne victory
at the Battle of the Little Bighorn, Sitting Bull led his
followers to Canada, at Alberta and Saskatchewan. His
band had alliances with bands of the Canadian Blackfeet
including the "Blood" and Siksika. The author retraced
the territory of Saskatoon, Moose Jaw, Wood Mountain
and Willow Bunch, Saskatchewan into the area of
present day Scobey, Montana, and south to Fort Peck
Indian Reservation on the old Sioux-Assiniboine Trail.
From the Fort Peck area the Poplar River connects with
the Missouri River and Sitting Bull's surrender route
would go east to Fort Buford near present Williston,
North Dakota. The trader at Willow Bunch, Jean Louis
Legare, was transporting those who were surrendering
to Fort Buford. He made several trips and would receive
compensation from the U.S. Government. Finally,
Sitting Bull would be among one of the travelers making
the trip. Throughout 1880 and early 1881 large numbers
of Lakota surrendered at Fort Buford including Gall,
Crow King, Low Dog, and Sitting Bull. Sitting Bull had
made a final plea to Canada for an agency (Reserve)
just before his surrender, but he was refused because
they said an agency for him was already appropriated
at Standing Rock. (Photo taken by D.F. Barry, c.
1884, postcard courtesy of Donovin Sprague.)

STEPS "NO FEET" (SHOSHONE-BANNOCK). Steps came to the
Nez Perce tribe as a slave. During this time he was punished for
a theft by having his feet and hands placed in iron animal traps
outside his owner's lodge. The temperature dropped to freezing
during the night and Step's two feet and one hand were frozen
off. Steps was freed after his debt was paid to his owner but
chose to stay with the Nez Perce. During the Nez Perce War
of 1877 Steps fought in the Big Hole and Bear's Paw battles.
During the Nez Perce flight to Canada, Steps made it to Canada
and lived with Sitting Bull's people until the Fort Buford
surrender in July 1881 and then moved to Standing Rock. In
later years Steps worked as a ranch hand in the Faith, S.D area
and displayed expert horsemanship skills. He trained and broke
horses and always carried his whip at his side. The Thomas
O'dell Collection contains letters written to O'dell in 1937 from
Mrs. Louise Sturgis about the character of Steps. Her brother Ed
hired Steps and he was described as a "mean man" who could
break any wild horse quickly but would sometimes use his whip
on people while on horseback. He wrapped rags around his legs
and waist area while mounted. He was let go as a ranch hand
because Ed accused Steps of using an herb to tame the wild
horses. The horses would later become wild again. (Photo taken
by D.F. Barry, courtesy of the Smithsonian Institute.)

GRAY EAGLE (HUNKPAPA). Gray Eagle stands by his tipi in this stereoview card with the American flag displayed. Gray Eagle was recognized for his knowledge and was greatly respected by the non-Indians. He wears a peace medal bestowed upon him by American government officials. Stereoview cards were used with a card holder to be viewed like the later "Viewmasters" and contain rare photos and scenes. (Photo taken by T.W. Ingersoll, 1899, stereoview card photo courtesy of Donovin Sprague.)

RAIN IN THE FACE (HUNKPAPA). Rain In The Face is pictured on his horse at Fort Yates, ND. Rain In The Face asked the photographer D.F. Barry to ask Governor John Miller of North Dakota to appoint Rain In The Face a policeman at the State Capital. The governor agreed but then rejected the appointment when he learned that Rain In The Face spoke no English. He would later learn a few English words and became an Indian policeman on the reservation. He also appears on crutches in other photos by Barry. This was from an injury sustained when he was in Canada and fell from his horse, when it stumbled while on a buffalo chase. Rain In The Face died on the Grand River in the Little Eagle, S.D. area on Sept. 12, 1905. (Photo taken by D.F. Barry, 1880s, photograph courtesy of Donovin Sprague.)

Four

TATANKA IYOTAKE NA CANK'PE OPI WICAKTEPI

(KILLING OF SITTING BULL AND WOUNDED KNEE)

SITTING BULL "TATANKA IYOTAKE" (HUNKPAPA). Sitting Bull learned to sign his autograph in English and did so many times during the Wild West Shows. He was known to have adopted many children into his family and had a lady friend Mary C. Collins, a missionary/doctor. She was given the name Winona and recorded historical information and photos of her life at Standing Rock. (Photo taken by Palmquist and Jurgens, 1884, postcard courtesy of Donovin Sprague.)

GRASS DANCERS AT FORT YATES, DAKOTA TERRITORY. This is a time of great transformation for the Hunkpapa with the start of the reservation era. (Photo taken by D.F. Barry, *c.* 1888, postcard courtesy of Donovin Sprague.)

SITTING BULL'S CABIN AT MCLAUGHLIN, S.D. Acting upon orders from Agent James McLaughlin, Indian Police entered this cabin on December 15, 1890 to arrest Sitting Bull, south of Bullhead, S.D. During the attempt to arrest him, Sitting Bull, his son Crow Foot, Sitting Bull's followers, and Indian Police were killed when a fight broke out and gunshots were exchanged. This cabin was moved from its original location to the McLaughlin City Park and was later taken to Chicago for an exposition. (Photo taken by Rinehart, 1898, photograph courtesy of Denver Public Library.)

SITTING BULL'S HORSE. This white horse was given to Sitting Bull as a gift by William F. "Buffalo Bill" Cody during the time that Sitting Bull participated in Buffalo Bill's Wild West Show. The horse was trained to rear up at the sound of gunshots for this show. When Sitting Bull was killed the horse went into its act in front of the slain body of its owner at the astonishment of onlookers. (Undated photo taken at Standing Rock Reservation, likely by Frank Fiske, courtesy of Melvin White Eagle and SHSND.)

SITTING BULL AND BUFFALO BILL CODY. Sitting Bull made one tour with William F. Cody's Wild West Show and was introduced to thousands of people. This photo is from that tour. Annie Oakley was also featured in the show as a sharpshooter. Earlier, in 1884, he had been allowed to leave the reservation to join Colonel Alvaren's Indian Exhibition and they toured 15 eastern U.S. cities. (Photo taken by David Notman, 1885, postcard courtesy of Donovin Sprague.)

CROW FOOT (HUNKPAPA). Crow Foot was the son of Sitting Bull and was born on the eve of the Battle of the Little Bighorn. He was named after a prominent Chief of the Blackfeet Nation (Siksika) in Canada who was a friend of Sitting Bull. Crow Foot would be next to his father during the 1881 surrender at Fort Buford, and would be killed at the age of fourteen along with his father when the arrest attempt was made by Indian police who entered their home while they were sleeping in bed on December 15, 1890. At Fort Buford Sitting Bull handed his rifle to Crow Foot to give to Major Brotherton. Sitting Bull then gave a surrender speech. (Photo likely by D.F. Barry c. 1880s, photograph courtesy of the Smithsonian Institute)

STANDING HOLY (HUNKPAPA). Standing Holy was the daughter of Sitting Bull and was born in 1876 while they were living in Montana. Sitting Bull enrolled his children into the Congregational Day School at Grand River. Following her father's death the surviving families would have their personal belongings searched, ransacked, and stolen from their homes. Her family left Standing Rock and she was raised on the Pine Ridge Indian Reservation. One Bull (nephew of Sitting Bull) and his family remained at Standing Rock. White Bull (nephew of Sitting Bull) and his family moved to Cheyenne River. The One Bull and White Bull descendants today come from a nephew bloodline of Sitting Bull. (Photo likely by D.F. Barry, c. 1885, photograph courtesy of the Smithsonian Institute.)

LEFT TO RIGHT: STANDING HOLY, SEEN BY HER NATION, WILLIAM SITTING BULL, LODGE IN SIGHT, AND HER FOUR ROBES (HUNKPAPA). Seen By Her Nation and Her Four Robes are wives of Sitting Bull. Their daughters here are Standing Holy and Lodge In Sight. The parents of Seen By Her Nation were Wiziogle and her mother Tiglagotawin. William Sitting Bull was the father of Nancy Kicking Bear. (Undated photo taken by D.F. Barry, courtesy of the Smithsonian Institute.)

SITTING BULL "TATANKA IYOTAKE" (HUNKPAPA). This photo was taken in later years of the life of Sitting Bull. A portrait was also made of him by German artist Rudolph Cronau at a meeting with Sitting Bull in the fall of 1881, shortly after the return from Canada. That fall he had been detained by the U.S. at Fort Randall in present southern South Dakota. Following this he would be transferred upriver to Standing Rock Agency. Rudolph Cronau was an artist and correspondent and with great fanfare he rushed to this site to meet Sitting Bull. On this visit to Standing Rock he also made a portrait of Rain In The Face (Hunkpapa) and Hump (Minnicoujou), who were also being detained. (Undated photograph courtesy of Denver Public Library.)

SIGNATURE DRAWING BY SITTING BULL. This is a drawing by Sitting Bull showing how he roped and captured a horse in Montana in 1866. The rider is Sitting Bull and the line from his mouth goes to a "sitting buffalo bull," hence you know this is Sitting Bull. This is how Sitting Bull depicted his name until he learned to write it in English. (Photograph courtesy of the Smithsonian Institute.)

NEW GRAVE SITE FOR SITTING BULL NEAR MOBRIDGE, S.D. This photo shows Sitting Bull's descendents, non-Indian land owners, and others in attendance for the dedication of the new location of the grave site of Sitting Bull. The family members are, from left to right, starting next to the man reading from the book, Clarence Grey Eagle, Angeline Spotted Horse LaPointe, Nancy Kicking Bear, Sarah Little Spotted Horse, Margaret One Bull/Tremmel, Claire "Regina" One Bull-Spotted Horse, and Jimmy White Bull. (April 1953 photograph courtesy of Ernie LaPointe and Ethel Bates.)

LEFT TO RIGHT: ROBERT SPOTTED HORSE (HUNKPAPA), ANGELINE SPOTTED HORSE LAPOINTE (HUNKPAPA), AND STANDING HOLY (HUNKPAPA). Standing Holy was a daughter of Sitting Bull and is with her children here visiting the marker and grave of Myrtle Ten Fingers. Myrtle's maiden name was Spotted Horse, and she was the oldest daughter of Standing Holy. Myrtle died in 1918. This area is near the White River, No. 6 Community, Red Shirt District. Robert and Angeline's parents were Urban Spotted Horse and Standing Holy. Urban's father was Hunts Enemy. This is not the same Hunts Enemy (Sword) who was Chief of Police at Pine Ridge. Robert Spotted Horse died during an epidemic of whooping cough and is buried at Oglala on Pine Ridge Indian Reservation. Standing Holy had 13 children and died in 1926 of tuberculosis. Her children included Myrtle, Robert, Eli, Isaac, Sarah, Angeline, Julia, Agnes, Alice, Cona, Josephine, Rufus, and Thomas. All the children preceded Standing Holy to the spirit world except for Angeline and Sarah. Standing Holy had a second husband named Black Wolf and a third husband was named All Around Fat, who was a Cheyenne River Lakota. All Around Fat also became known as Amos Little; he survived Standing Holy but they had no children. There were also no children from the marriage of Black Wolf and Standing Holy. (Photo taken at Pine Ridge Indian Reservation, c. 1920, courtesy of Ernie LaPointe and Ethel Bates.)

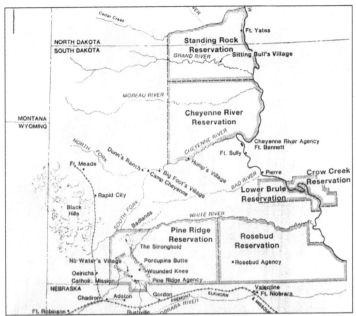

MAP OF LAKOTA RESERVATIONS, 1890. At the top is the Standing Rock Reservation and the other Lakota reservations to the south. (Map courtesy of Donovin Sprague.)

WOUNDED KNEE MASSACRE SITE. This is the front entrance to the mass grave site where the bodies of the victims of the December 29th, 1890 Wounded Knee Massacre were buried without ceremony, all in one pit and stacked upon each other. Following the killing of Sitting Bull on December 15, 1890 Ghost Dancers fled from Standing Rock to Chief Hump's camp at Cherry Creek on Cheyenne River Reservation, where Ghost Dancing was being done. Nelson Miles sent a messenger to Hump to ask him to go into Fort Bennett on Cheyenne River. He did this and brought in a large band, however some joined the nearby camp of Si Tanka (Big Foot) in the Takini and Bridger area where they went south to Pine Ridge Indian Reservation to see Red Cloud. About 300 were killed in the well known massacre that involved mostly Si Tanka's Minnicoujou's and Standing Rock Hunkpapa's, as well as Cheyenne River bands the Itazipco, Siha Sapa, and Oohenumpa. The author also talked to family members from Standing Rock who had Yanktonai family in the massacre. Wounded Knee marks the end of America's "wars" with the American Indians, 113 years ago. (Photograph taken in 2002 courtesy of Donovin Sprague.)

Five

INYAN WOSLATA
(STANDING ROCK RESERVATION)

1900–1950s

STANDING ROCK AGENCY, FORT YATES, N.D. Prior to the military post coming to Fort Yates, it was a community populated by the Lakota/Dakota/Nakota tribes. The Lewis and Clark Expedition stayed several days in this vicinity in the winter of 1803. By 1819 steamboat travel reached the Upper Missouri and by 1860 regular steamboat traffic brought adventurers and settlers to this community. Standing Rock Agency was defined by treaty in 1868 and the military post was established. By 1870 there were 540 Sioux living at Fort Yates, with great numbers ignoring Agency orders to surrender at the fort. Many were engaging in warfare against non-Indian encroachment on their lands. In 1873 Fort Yates moved to this present site and Agency buildings were constructed. Prior to this the Agency was the Grand River Agency in present Corson County, S.D. Agent Cady wrote in 1871 that it was not a good site because of flooding. The Agency then moved north to this location though military forces were left at Grand River until a transition occurred and they relocated here. In this photo a caption reads that the ice is breaking up on the Missouri River and this is the highest water level ever known. In 2003 the river was at one of the lowest levels that many have seen. (Photo taken by Frank Fiske, March 15, 1910.)

STANDING ROCK DELEGATION TO WASHINGTON, DC. These are the members of a delegation which visited Washington, DC from the Standing Rock Agency. From left to right are: (front row) High Bear, Thunder Hawk, Bear's Rib, Hairy Chin (standing at center with Pipe), Walking Eagle (or Black Animal "Prairie" Dog), and Gray Eagle;(middle row) Big Head, Gall, John Grass, and Fire Heart; (back row) Louis Primeau (or Louis Duncan) (interpreter), High Eagle, and Stephen Two Bears. The photographer was not recorded, but could have been T.W. Smillie. The exact date of the photo is thought to be October, 15, 1888. The photo was in a file of the Oscar Huettner Collection. The photo is also available without the numbers attached on their hats. Others who were part of this group but not photographed were, Mad Bear, Sitting Bull, and Agent James McLaughlin. Mad Bear was ill and Sitting Bull was left out of sight, avoiding the photograph. Hairy Chin is present but also shows his disapproval of policy by holding the Pipe upside down. (Photo taken Oct. 1888, courtesy of Klein Museum, Mobridge, S.D.)

ST. PETERS CATHOLIC CHURCH. In this photo priests are entering the church at Fort Yates, N.D. (Photo likely by Fiske, June 25th, 1910, courtesy of Timber Lake and Area Historical Society.)

Wakpala, S.D. This photo was taken in present Wakpala, S.D. and shows two log cabin dwellings, a tipi, and a soldier tent. (Photo taken in 1908, courtesy of Oscar Huettner Collection, Klein Museum, Mobridge, S.D.)

Henry Lawrence (Standing Rock). Henry Lawrence is seated on the right, and the other man with chaps of wool is unidentified. Both are Standing Rock Sioux cowboys at Fort Yates. (Photo taken by Fiske, *c.* 1910, postcard courtesy of Donovin Sprague.)

RIFLEMEN AT STANDING ROCK. The caption with the photo reads "The gang at the Turkey Shoot, which was held on the day before Thanksgiving. Under the auspices of The Federation of Crack Shots of Standing Rock." (Undated photograph courtesy of Timber Lake and Area Historical Society.)

BULLHEAD, S.D. The original name for Bullhead was Inyan Cunkaske which meant Rock Corral. Mr. James Yellow Earrings, Sr. related this story: "About nine miles north of Bullhead, a band of Sioux had a summer campsite. Indians from a different tribe came to this campsite on a raiding party. Before they had a chance to raid or steal horses, they were discovered and killed inside a rock corral." The remains of old "Inyan Cunkaske" is still evident on Rock Creek, which flows through the community, dividing it into east and west sides. Bullhead was later named for Lt. Bull Head, captain of the Indian police, who was killed in the Sitting Bull fight in 1890. This killing took place south of Bullhead near the Grand River. (Photo likely by Fiske, undated, courtesy of Joe Laundreaux and Timber Lake and Area Historical Society.)

NORTHERN LAKOTA CHILDREN. These "two of a kind" girls hold boxes of Uneeda Biscuits. The dress yokes are dentalium shell, a trade item. The postcard was produced by the Timber Lake and Area Historical Society. (Undated photo taken by Frank Cundill, postcard courtesy of Donovin Sprague.)

HARRY BICKEL, WHITE PLUME, AND OTHERS. These people are gathered for a Sunday picnic along Firesteel Creek shortly before the Holy Spirit Church was built. Harry Bickel and White Plume are sitting beside the tent by the buggy. Harry is the grandfather of Jack Bickel, who provided the photo. (Undated photo taken at Firesteel Creek, S.D by Waffle Studio, courtesy of Jack Bickel.)

OLD STONE CHURCH. This Episcopal Church is between Bullhead and Firesteel, S.D. and was called the Chapel of the Holy Spirit. It is on the National Register of Historic Sites. It was built of beautiful stone from a nearby butte and was finished in 1923 under the direction of Frank Waggoner of Keldron, S.D. (Undated photograph courtesy of Timber Lake and Area Historical Society.)

UNIDENTIFIED WINYAN (WOMAN). This photo was probably taken in Huettner's studio in Mobridge, S.D. (Undated photo from the Oscar Huettner Collection, courtesy of Klein Museum, Mobridge, S.D.)

ABRAHAM BLACK SHIELD/AKA LONE WOLF (SIHA SAPA). Black Shield was on the 1876 Standing Rock Census and later moved to Cheyenne River Reservation where Abraham is enrolled. Abraham was born in 1849 and married Her White Horse, who was born in 1850. Their children were Edith Black Shield (born in 1881), Wallace Brings The Horses/aka Wallace Black Shield (born in 1885), and Ida Black Shield (born in 1886). The parents of Abraham were Black Shield (Wakacanka Sapa) his father, and Rattling Track. Rattling Track records show she was aka Esther Wind Woman, daughter of Red Hair – Elk Head, a keeper of the Sacred Buffalo Calf Pipe at Green Grass, S.D. on the Cheyenne River. Abraham's father was a signer of the 1868 Treaty of Fort Laramie and was listed as a headman of the Siha Sapa. He was killed at the Wounded Knee Massacre in 1890. Abraham was a U.S. Scout and his paternal grandfather was Lone Wolf, so Abraham also used this family name. He also had a marriage to Cross Woman. A friend of the author is Catherine Brings The Horses/ Silva and her father was Wallace Brings The Horses, the son of Abraham. Wallace was born at Green Grass, S.D. Catherine's husband, James Holy Eagle, lived to the age of 102. (Undated photo taken by Frank Cundill, courtesy of Timber Lake and Area Historical Society.)

WILLIAM BUCKNER'S FIRST WIFE AND FAMILY? This photo was thought to be of William Buckner's first wife. The man and child are not identified. In family notes William Buckner was at Fort Lincoln with Custer and William's wife sewed ball gowns for Mrs. Elizabeth Custer. She is pictured here but her name is not known; she is the great grandmother of Carole Kloss. (Undated photo possibly by R.L. Kelly Studio of Pierre, S.D., courtesy of Carole Kloss.)

GROUP NEAR FORT YATES, N.D. Sioux Indian performances were held for passengers traveling on the Olympian and Columbian trains. The large boulder rocks are from the nearby Cannon Ball River which gets its name from the round limestone formations rolled in shape by the river and its bed. Once there were many rocks but people took most of them away. Cannon Ball is a very historic village and goes back to the early 1700s, and Lewis and Clark were among early non-Indian visitors. Later, Cannon Ball had stagecoach, steamboat and railroad traffic because of its close location to Fort Rice. At Solen, N.D. the Northern Pacific depot agent was housed in a red railroad box car in 1915. Early depot agents were Cecil Crandell, Mr. Bohlig, and Mrs. Walter Higgins. (Undated photo from the Huettner Collection, courtesy of Klein Museum, Mobridge, S.D.)

ST. ELIZABETH'S EPISCOPAL CHURCH 50TH DEDICATION, WAKPALA, S.D. A large number of people attended the 50th Anniversary dedication of the St. Elizabeth's Episcopal Church near Wakpala. The church is in the background and still looks the same today. It was erected in 1885. (Photo from Oscar Huettner, taken in 1935, courtesy of Klein Museum, Mobridge, S.D.)

STANDING ROCK GROUP. Pictured from left to right are: (front row) Mrs. Carry Moccasin, Mrs. His White Horse, Bear Soldier, His White Horse, Fire Cloud, and Mule Bear; (back row) Paul Long Bull, Good Dog, Rev. Thomas Blue Eyes (Minnicoujou), Long Feather, Henry Oscar One Bull, Joe Has Horns, Zahn, and Usher Burdick. Most of the group here are Hunkpapa or Yanktonai. Mr. Burdick published some historical research, including "Tales From Buffalo Land." (Undated photo taken by Frank Fiske, courtesy of State Historical Society of North Dakota #7387.)

LEFT TO RIGHT: BEN LONEMAN, MRS. CECELIA BULLHEAD, MRS. FRANCES ARCHAMBAULT, AND MRS. CAROLINA RED HORSE. (Undated photo taken by Frank Fiske, courtesy of SHSND Fiske 4027.)

PARADE IN NORTH DAKOTA. This photo is entitled "Sioux Indians On Parade in North Dakota." The man at the far right carries an American flag. The photo could be from the 1940s era or earlier. (Undated postcard courtesy of *McLaughlin Messenger*.)

SAM BRUGUIER AND WAGON. Sam Bruguier is shown here in the lead wagon drawn by a team of horses. He is transporting chairs and property from the Little Eagle, S.D. school. Sam was born in 1854 at Fort Yates, N.D. (Undated photo by Fiske, postcard courtesy of *McLaughlin Messenger*.)

JAMES BLUE STONE (STANDING ROCK).
(Photo taken by R.L. Kelly, Pierre, S.D.,
courtesy of Brenda Red Tomahawk.)

**LEFT TO RIGHT: SOPHIE
ARCHAMBAULT, SUSAN BULLHEAD,
AND JOHN ARCHAMBAULT (SITTING ON
SUSAN'S KNEE) (FRENCH/HUNKPAPA).**
Susan Bullhead was one of three wives
of Hermides H.A. "Harry" Archambault,
Sr. and is pictured here with two of
their children, Sophie and John. H.A.
"Harry" was French and had a store at
Thunder Hawk, S.D. Germaine Eagle
of Bullhead, S.D. assisted the author
and is the 76 year old daughter of John
Archambault and Margaret Little Eagle.
There are two Sophie Archambaults at
Standing Rock. (Undated photograph
courtesy of Germaine Eagle.)

ROBERT "FATS" MCLAUGHLIN (LEFT) AND WILLIAM LITTLE BIRD (STANDING ROCK). This picture was taken in front of a tent at a celebration in Fort Yates, N.D. (Undated photograph courtesy of Brenda Red Tomahawk.)

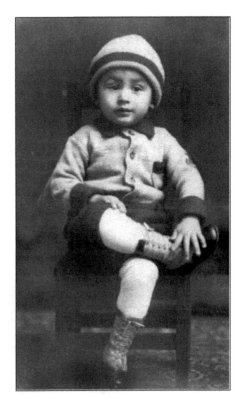

COLLINS S. LAMONTE (HUNKPAPA). Collins LaMonte was born in Wakpala, S.D. in 1916 and married Bertha Huber. Collins' parents were Edward S. LaMonte and Anna D. Buckner. The grandparents of Collins LaMonte were John LaMonte and Cecelia LaMonte. Collins daughter Carole LaMonte Kloss submitted the photo, and she was born at Fort Yates, N.D. and now lives in California. (Photo taken *c.* 1913, courtesy of Carole Kloss.)

ARMSTRONG FOUR BEAR (OOHENUMPA).
Armstrong was a showman as a Lakota
cowboy and trick roper. He was born in
1889 and married Jennie Meeter in 1921.
He entertained many people at Standing
Rock and Cheyenne River, where he has
family at both reservations. He traveled
extensively and performed for the King
and Queen of England. His parents were
Thomas Crow Eagle Sand and Louise Four
Bear. He passed away in 1970 at the age
of 81. This postcard was developed by the
Timber Lake and Area Historical Society.
(Undated photo taken by Frank Cundill,
courtesy of Donovin Sprague.)

**MR. AND MRS. JOE TWIN "CEKPA"
(STANDING ROCK).** Joseph Cekpa Twin
was born in 1870 at Fort Yates and married
his wife Rhabana in 1893. Rhabana
was born in 1872. A child of theirs was
named Ruth Twin who was born on
November 26, 1895. (Undated photograph
courtesy of Donovin Sprague.)

FORT YATES ALTAR BOYS. This group of altar boys was photographed at the Catholic Church on Christmas, December 25, 1904. Pictured from left to right are: (first row) Henry White Bird, James Hollow, John Spotted Bird, Philip Bull Head, Mike Halsey, and Joe Two Bull; (second row) White Bird, Tom Pheasant, Leo Archambault, Joe White Bird, George Halsey, Ed Meny, John Archambault, Barney Red Tomahawk, Alec Travery, Sidney McLaughlin, and Two Bull; (third row) Francis Zahn, Fr. Francis, John Shave Bear, and Ben Cloud. (Photo taken by Fiske, 1904, courtesy of Melvin White Eagle and SHSND.)

(HENRY) OSCAR ONE BULL AND FAMILY (HUNKPAPA). Oscar and his wife are in the center surrounded by their son in law, daughter, and grandchildren in the front. (Photo taken 1937, courtesy of South Dakota State Archives.)

LEFT TO RIGHT: UNIDENTIFIED, MOSES BRAVE, RAYMOND HAIRY CHIN, AND ANDREW DEROCKBRAINE. Members of the Standing Rock Tribe were selected as actors and extras in the Hollywood film *They Died With Their Boots On*, which portrayed the Battle of the Little Bighorn. (Photo taken in late 1940s, courtesy of Melvin White Eagle and SHSND.)

(LEFT): SUSAN MARY POWER & (RIGHT): JOSEPHINE GATES KELLY (YANKTONAI). Josephine is the granddaughter of Chief Two Bear and was the first American Indian woman to become Tribal Chairwoman. Susan Mary Power is Josephine's granddaughter and today is a Harvard University Law School graduate and author. (Photograph courtesy of Susan Kelly Power.)

THREE WICASA (MEN). The three men in this photo from the Oscar Huetter Collection are unidentified. (Undated photograph courtesy of Klein Museum, Mobridge, S.D.)

WAKPALA HIGH SCHOOL 1930-31 BOYS BASKETBALL TEAM. The Wakpala Sioux are pictured here with two team trophies. Is this your lala/tunkasila, ate, leksi, tahansi, kola, or nis? The author participated in basketball games at the school, which sadly was recently destroyed by fire. (Photo from Oscar Huettner Collection, taken 1930-31, courtesy of Klein Museum, Mobridge, S.D.)

WAKPALA SIOUX BASKETBALL TEAM. This photo appears to be taken in front of the old school at Wakpala, S.D. Pictured from left to right are: (front row) Sidney Eagle Shield, Sr., Joe Eagle Man, and unidentified; (back row) Eli Spotted Horse, Matt One Feather, Leo Chasing Hawk, Clayton Many Deeds, and Percy Uses Arrow. (Undated photograph courtesy of Bill and Maryann Helper and *Teton Times*.)

SAM CADOTTE (HUNKPAPA). Sam Cadotte is shown here on a wild buffalo ride at a rodeo. He was known for his rodeo skills such as this, and Gene Cadotte of McLaughlin, S.D. is a son of his and his daughters are Daisy Mae LeCompte of California and Violet Cadotte of Bismarck, N.D. It was said that Sam broke his leg, possibly on this ride. (Undated photo taken by Frank Fiske, courtesy of SHSND Fiske 5258.)

ELIZA JANE HOWARD STANDING BEAR (STANDING ROCK). Eliza married Luke Eagleman, Jr. and they had five girls and one son. Their daughter Charmayne Eagleman lives at Wakpala and submitted this photo that was taken at Wakpala, S.D. The Hu-Mo (Huettner) Photo Service of Mobridge, S.D. developed the picture. (Photo taken July 25, 1937, courtesy of Charmayne Eagleman.)

HENRY "OSCAR" ONE BULL "TATANKA WANJILA" (HUNKPAPA). One Bull is pictured here in later years, believed to be near Cherry Creek, S.D. Makes Room was the father of One Bull and White Bull. (Undated photograph courtesy of Donovin Sprague.)

MOBRIDGE, S.D. PARADE. Mobridge, S.D. is the closest larger town across the Missouri River from the Standing Rock Sioux Reservation, with a population of just over 4,000 people. It is also close to the Cheyenne River Sioux Reservation. Oscar Huettner had a photography studio in town and took pictures of early settlement of the city and surrounding area in the early 1920s. Many of the pictures are from the Wakpala area and the dedication of the Mobridge Auditorium on May 6–8, 1937. Oscar Huettner either took the photos or they were in his collection. (Photo from Oscar Huettner Collection, c. late 1920s, courtesy of Klein Museum, Mobridge, S.D.)

UNIDENTIFIED TIWAHE (FAMILY). (Undated photo from Oscar Huettner Collection, courtesy of Klein Museum, Mobridge, S.D.)

UNIDENTIFIED WINYAN (WOMAN). (Undated Photo from Oscar Huettner Collection, courtesy of Klein Museum, Mobridge, S.D.)

STANDING ROCK CAMP. The photo shows the traditional tipi with a man standing next to it as well as a man sits under the shade area. Visible transitional items shown are iron kettles, pans, a buckboard wagon, cowboy hats, a chair, and the log cabin dwelling in back. (Undated photo from Oscar Huettner Collection, courtesy of Klein Museum, Mobridge, S.D.)

STANDING ROCK CAMP. Photo from Oscar Huettner Collection, undated. This camp is thought to be at Fort Yates, N.D. (Photograph courtesy of Klein Museum, Mobridge, S.D.)

UNIDENTIFIED MEN. These men are in the Huettner studio in Mobridge, S.D. (Undated photo from Oscar Huettner Collection, courtesy of Klein Museum, Mobridge, S.D.)

BLACK CROW "KANGI SAPA" (LAKOTA) AND LITTLE GIRL. This photo was taken at Mobridge, S.D. The Black Crow name appears at Standing Rock, Cheyenne River, and Pine Ridge. (Undated photo from Oscar Huettner Collection, courtesy of Klein Museum, Mobridge, S.D.)

UNIDENTIFIED MAN AND TWO WOMEN (LAKOTA). (Undated photograph from Oscar Huettner Collection, courtesy of Klein Museum, Mobridge, S.D.)

UNIDENTIFIED GROUP OF FOUR MEN. This photo looks like it was taken in the Huettner studio in Mobridge, S.D. (Undated photo from Oscar Huettner Collection, courtesy of Klein Museum, Mobridge, S.D.)

RAMONA WAGGONER SKOGEN (HUNKPAPA). Ramona was the daughter of author and historian Josephine McCarty Waggoner and John Franklin Waggoner. Ramona's daughter was Josephine Braine Fuhrman, whose husband Chester Fuhrman provided the photo. (Undated photograph courtesy of Chester Fuhrman.)

89

(*above*) **PRESIDENT HARRY S. TRUMAN AND TWO UNIDENTIFIED MEN.** It was thought that maybe Truman came to the Mobridge area. However, the author spoke to elder Jim Byington of Mobridge who attended the dedication of the Mobridge Auditorium in 1937 (before Truman's presidency) and he said that Truman was not there but the Lawrence Welk Orchestra did play for two or three nights. The author also contacted Ken Stewart at the South Dakota Archives and their records indicate that Truman never visited South Dakota. The next contact was with the North Dakota Archives, where it was learned that Truman

made a train "whistle stop tour" through North Dakota in 1950–1952 to Williston, Minot, New Rockford, and Fargo. He also returned to Minot as ex-president in 1958. None of these cities are close to the Standing Rock Reservation and photographer Huettner could have photographed tribes to the north. The man in the center could be a Lakota/Dakota/Nakota Itancan (leader). (Undated photo from Oscar Huettner Collection, courtesy of Klein Museum, Mobridge, S.D.)

(*left*) **UNIDENTIFIED WOMAN AT MOBRIDGE, S.D.** This woman is believed to have participated in the dedication ceremonies of the Mobridge, S.D. City Auditorium in 1937 and she is pictured in front of the building in traditional dress. Oscar Howe, a well known Yanktonai artist and educator, painted the cultural murals in the auditorium, and also the murals in the Corn Palace in Mitchell, S.D. He was raised and began his education at Crow Creek Reservation, S.D. (Photo from Huettner Collection, May 1937, courtesy of Klein Museum, Mobridge, S.D.)

SAMUEL STANDING BEAR (HUNKPAPA). It was recalled by Wakpala, S.D. residents that Samuel Standing Bear lived down along Oak Creek and it was thought that the name of his wife was Julia. He journeyed to the spirit world in 1939. (Undated photo from Oscar Huettner Collection, courtesy of Klein Museum, Mobridge, S.D.)

SIOUX COUNTY PIONEER MARCH. Robert Bruce (Standing Rock) was a Sioux County Indian musician who played in the Million Dollar Band and Sousa's Band. He wrote "The Sioux County Pioneer March" and this is the sheet music for the song. It was published by Robert Bruce "Najinyampi" of McLaughlin, S.D. and the march was dedicated to Mr. C. Christianson of Fort Yates, N.D. Robert Bruce married Ms. Gayton, daughter of James B. Gayton. Robert lived until 1921. (Photograph courtesy of Sioux County History Book staff.)

CLAUDE LaPOINTE. (DAKOTA/ FRENCH) AND ANGELINE SPOTTED HORSE LaPOINTE (HUNKPAPA). Claude and Angeline are seated in front of their second home and Angeline was ill at this time. The parents of Claude were Jacob LaPointe and Gertie White Rabbit. (Photo taken in Rapid City, S.D. *c.* 1959, courtesy of Ernie LaPointe and Ethel Bates.)

JOSEPHINE HILDERMAN FUHRMAN (HUNKPAPA). Josephine "Ishto To To" (Blue Eyes) was born in 1916 at Keldron, S.D. to Alfred "Scotty" and Ramona Waggoner Braine. She worked for the Dept. of Health, Education, and Welfare for 31 years, retiring in 1975 after serving the people of the Crow and Northern Cheyenne tribes as a Nurse in the IHS Hospital at Crow Agency. Josephine's grandmother was Josephine Waggoner, a well known Lakota historian and author. Josephine's survivors include her husband Chester Fuhrman of Hardin, Montana. (Undated photograph courtesy of Chester Fuhrman, Jr.)

Six

OKOLAKICIYE AKICITA
(SOLDIER SOCIETY/VETERANS)

133: SIOUX SURVIVORS OF THE BATTLE OF THE LITTLE BIG HORN (CUSTER'S LAST STAND)

Little Warrior   Pemmican   Little Soldier   Dewey Beard   John Sitting Bull   High Eagle   Iron Hawk   Comes Again

BATTLE OF THE LITTLE BIGHORN SURVIVORS. This photograph was taken in the Black Hills of South Dakota, at a reunion of some known survivors of the famous battle that took place 72 years earlier. Pictured, from left to right, are: Little Warrior, Pemmican, Little Soldier, Dewey Beard, John Sitting Bull, High Eagle, Iron Hawk, and Comes Again. The postcard says that they are all "Oglala Sioux survivors," but at least three are not Oglala. Little Soldier was Yanktonai, John Sitting Bull was Hunkpapa, and Dewey Beard "Iron Hail" is Minnicoujou. The photographer, Bill Groethe, is a friend of the author and operates a photo studio in Rapid City, S.D. He took the picture and is now 80 years old and stated that the original negative of this postcard was not returned and is lost. A postcard business later added color to the photograph. (Photo taken by Bill Groethe, 1948, postcard courtesy of Donovin Sprague.)

DOUGH BOY STATUE, BULLHEAD, S.D.
The Dough Boy statue was erected at Bullhead on June 28, 1935 to honor the service of the Dough Boys of World War I. It is very honorable to be a Lakota warrior and serve the people of the United States. (Photo taken in 2003, courtesy of Donovin Sprague.)

UNIDENTIFIED MEN. Pictured here are two unidentified men. The man standing is an Indian policeman, probably photographed in the Huettner studio in Mobridge, S.D. (Undated photo from the Oscar Huettner Collection, courtesy of Klein Museum, Mobridge, S.D.)

RED TOMAHAWK (LEFT) AND EAGLE
MAN. Both are Hunkpapa families,
and the Eagle Man family is listed
under Thunder Hawk's band in the
1876 Standing Rock Census. The
photo was possibly taken by D.F. Barry
in the 1880s. The men are pictured
here in their Indian police uniforms
with their weapons. The Indian police
would participate in the attempted
arrest and killing of Sitting Bull and
his followers. (Photograph courtesy
of the Smithsonian Institute.)

JUDGE CRAZY WALKING (STANDING
ROCK). Crazy Walking was appointed
to the position of Judge of the Indian
Court of Offenses following the death
of Gall and John Grass, who had
previously served. Prior to this, Crazy
Walking was a Captain of the Indian
police at Standing Rock. (Photo taken
by D.F. Barry in the 1880s, courtesy of
the Smithsonian Institute.)

MARY TASINA MANI CRAWLER AKA MOVING ROBE WOMAN (HUNKPAPA). Mary was born in 1854 and participated in the Battle of the Little Bighorn in 1876 when she was 22 years old. She gave valuable testimony on battle participants and activity, especially near the area of Last Stand Hill where Custer and his soldiers met their defeat. Rain In The Face said Moving Robe had a brother who was killed just before the Custer fight against Three Stars. This would be General Crook's defeat at the Battle of the Rosebud with about 1,000 soldiers, by the Lakota and Cheyenne. At the Greasy Grass (Little Bighorn), Moving Robe carried her brother's war staff and led a charge against the soldiers. She later took the name of Mary. Her father's name was Slohan (Crawler). Mary was the wife of a Hunkpapa warrior, and adopted Fanny Kelly, who was taken as a wife for Brings Plenty. Brings Plenty was an Oglala who traded for Fanny Kelly, a Shetak captive taken by the Santee (Dakota) in the 1862 Minnesota conflict. Mary Crawler made Fanny Kelly her sister and brought her into the family. Mary was from Kenel, S.D., a community named for Father Martin Kenel. (Undated photo likely by Fiske, courtesy of Donovin Sprague.)

ED LEAN ELK, ALBERT GRASS, BEN GRAY HAWK, AND ALBERT AFRAID OF HAWK. This picture reads that this group is leaving Standing Rock so Ben Gray Hawk could join the U.S. Army. The driver is Ed Lean Elk, and the passenger in the front seat is Albert Grass. Ben and his cousin Albert Afraid Of Hawk are in the back seat, but the photo caption does not specify on which side. Albert Grass would lose his life in the war. (Photo taken March 29, 1918, courtesy of Melvin White Eagle and SHSN.D.)

EDGAR ARCHAMBAULT (STANDING ROCK).
This photo was taken at Exretat, France.
Edgar is standing in the middle, in the back
row. He was a paratrooper with the 101st
Airbourne Division of the U.S. Army and
posed for this picture on his way to England.
Edgar is the brother of Germaine Eagle of
Bullhead, S.D. and is the father of Sharon
Archambault No Heart of Rapid City, S.D.
The other soldiers are unidentified. (Undated
photograph courtesy of Germaine Eagle.)

PARADE OF LAKOTA'S AT MCLAUGHLIN, S.D. The people are unidentified at this McLaughlin, S.D. downtown parade in which the Lakota man displays the American flag, probably at a Fourth of July event. The city was established in 1908 and was named for Standing Rock Agent Major James McLaughlin and his family. Major McLaughlin became the agent in 1881 and at this time there were bands of Hunkpapa, Yanktonai, Siha Sapa, Minnicoujou, Itazipco, Oglala, and Sicangu living in the Standing Rock area. (Undated postcard courtesy of *McLaughlin Messenger*.)

CHARLES FOOL BEAR, JR. (STANDING ROCK). Charles Fool Bear, Jr. is from Cannon Ball District and is shown here as a sailor in the U.S. Navy. (Undated photograph courtesy of Brenda Red Tomahawk.)

TIPI AND AMERICAN FLAG. This could be part of a July 4th celebration. Native Americans have the highest rate of enlistment into the U.S. military of any group of people, and 50 percent of Native Americans are veterans. It is very good to be a Lakota/Dakota/Nakota warrior. (Undated photo from Oscar Huettner Collection, courtesy of Klein Museum, Mobridge, S.D.)

Seven

OWAYAWA EL' TIPI
(BOARDING SCHOOLS)

CARLISLE INDIAN SCHOOL, PA CLASSROOM. Many American Indian students were sent to Carlisle Indian School in Pennsylvania. This photo shows a classroom of girls whose organization was called the "Longstreth Literacy Society." As the quote on the wall reads ("Labor Conquers All Things"), hard labor was a requirement and an important school ethic for every student. The schools founder was Captain Pratt and he is pictured on the wall below the word "Conquers." (Photo by Frances Benjamin Johnston, 1902, courtesy of Cumberland County Historical Society, Carlisle, PA.)

PHILIP FROSTED (YANKTONAI). This photo was labeled as "Philip Frosted in Hampden uniform," which refers to Hampton Institute. Hampton records show Thomas Frost attended the school from 1885–1887 and Philip attended around this time also. Many students also attended Haskell Institute in Kansas in later years. The students were required to dress in military style uniforms. (Undated photo taken by Frank Fiske, courtesy of SHSND Fiske 2198.)

ROSA BEAR FACE (STANDING ROCK). Rosa was the first school teacher at Fort Yates. Rosa is listed as a student in the Hampton Institute records in Virginia. Her Lakota name is listed as Topala and she attended during the school years 1881-1884 when she was 17 years old, and later during the 1887-1888 school year at age 22. Her father is listed as Bear Face from Standing Rock. Rosa's brother was named Armstrong Four Bear (Oohenumpa); he was a prolific entertainer in rodeo and roping. Armstrong Four Bear was the stepfather of Gladys Hawk (Hunkpapa), of Wakpapa, S.D. (Undated photograph courtesy of Melvin White Eagle and SHSND.)

1930 Standing Rock Boarding School Eighth Grade Graduates. Pictured from left to right are: (front row) Ambrose Dog Eagle, Clementine Spotted Horse, Margaret Walker, Minnie Earth Eater, and Frank Shooter; (back row) George Archambault, Marie Antelope, Jennie Four Swords, Ed Vermillion, and Charles Snow. Some of the communities these students came from include Little Eagle, Cannon Ball, Bullhead, Fort Yates, and Kenel. (Photo taken by Frank Fiske in 1930 at Fort Yates, N.D., courtesy of SHSND Fiske 7602.)

Minnie? Deloria (left) and Ella C. Deloria (Yankton). Ella C. Deloria and Minnie Deloria were the daughters of Philip Deloria, Sr. and Mary Deloria. The back of this picture is labeled "Ella C. Deloria and "ynia? C. Deloria." Ella's Indian name was "Anpetu Waste Win" (Beautiful Day Woman). Ella is remembered as an educator and author. She was born in 1889 at White Swan-Lake Andes, S.D. on the Yankton Sioux Reservation. Ella spent her formative years with the Hunkpapa and Siha Sapa at Standing Rock Reservation and graduated from Columbia University. She collaborated with Franz Boas on three books; *Dakota Texts* (1932), *Dakota Grammar* (1941), and *Speaking of Indians* (1944). *Buffalo People* and *Waterlily* are two later books by Ella. Their father, Philip Sr., was an Episcopal minister. Ella was the third daughter of Philip and the first child of his marriage to Mary Sully Bordeaux. After Ella, two more children were born to Philip and Mary, a daughter, Susan Mabel, and a son, Vine Victor Deloria. Bea Medicine is a well known educator and author who studied the writings of Ella. (Undated photograph courtesy of Carole Kloss.)

WILLIAM LITTLEBIRD AKA ISAAC THIGH (HUNKPAPA). This photo was taken while William Littlebird was at the Bismarck Indian School. His parents were John Thigh (Little Bird) and (Ropena) Mrs. Thigh/Mrs. Sarah Little Bird. John Thigh was born in 1861 and lived until 1933. John's father's name has been lost but his mother's name was Her Black Door. Mrs. Thigh's father was Tobacco Mouth who was born in 1820 and her mother is unknown, as this is long before land allotment records. William Littlebird was the great uncle of Brenda Red Tomahawk, but was referred to as her Lala (Grandpa) in the Lakota way. William "Bill" gave historic interviews about his family and tribe in 1980 at Fort Yates, N.D. He was born in Cannon Ball, N.D. on November 16, 1902. For over 50 years he lived in the Cannon Ball District. (Photo taken at Bismarck, N.D., June 19, 1921, courtesy of Brenda Red Tomahawk.)

ANNE BUCKNER (LAMONTE) AND MARTIN KENEL SCHOOL EMPLOYEES. Employees of the Martin Kenel School at Standing Rock are shown in this picture. Anna Buckner (LaMonte) is pictured in the center, seated with a hat. Anna was a cook at the school, and was the grandmother of Carole Kloss, who provided the photo. (Photo taken in 1913, courtesy of Carole Kloss.)

Eight

WOUNSPE TECA
(NEW EDUCATION)

STANDING ROCK COMMUNITY COLLEGE BOARD OF TRUSTEES. Pictured from left to right are Charles Murphy, Gladys Hawk, Joe White Mountain, Sr., Geraldine Agard, Ambrose Dog Eagle, Joe Keeps Eagle, and Clayton Brown Otter (Board President). (Photo taken at Fort Yates, N.D., *c.* 1982, courtesy of Sitting Bull College.)

TEACHER TRAINING PROGRAM. Pictured from left to right are Candy Luger, Unidentified, Velia Salas, Cordell Morsette, Margaret Teach Out, Earl Vermillion, E.J. Blue Earth (in white outfit with her back to camera), and Jim Shanley (in dark suit with back to camera). Jim Shanley, the President, and E.J. Blue Earth, a board member, are presenting college graduates with certificates at the powwow grounds. The students are unidentified. (Photo taken at Fort Yates, N.D., May 1980, courtesy of Sitting Bull College.)

LAUREL VERMILLION AND FERDINAND TWIN (HUNKPAPA). Laurel is now Vice President of Sitting Bull College. Ferdinand is the student in the photo (No. 10 on shirt), and is the son of Walter Twin. (Photo taken in 1978, courtesy of Sitting Bull College.)

COLLEGE CEREMONY. Pictured from left to right are Kerwin Lindstrom, Pat McLaughlin, Jim Shanley, E.J. Blue Earth, Gary Rush (tall man in back of E.J.), Unidentified woman, Alice Voorhees (dressed in white and looking at camera), and Jan Murry. The others are unidentified. Joe Flying Bye is the speaker with the microphone. Joe is now deceased. (Photo taken c. 1975, courtesy of Sitting Bull College.)

LEFT TO RIGHT: UNIDENTIFIED, ALICE VOORHEES, ARTHUR AMIOTTE (OGLALA), JOE FLYING BYE (HUNKPAPA), BILL GREY BULL, AND MRS. GREY BULL (STANDING ROCK). This photo was taken at a Sitting Bull College ceremony. The author was part of the university faculty with Alice Voorhees and her husband Dr. Rick Voorhees at Black Hills State University in Spearfish, S.D. in the early 1990s. (Photo taken c. 1975, courtesy of Sitting Bull College.)

FRANK LAWRENCE AND UNIDENTIFIED MAN. Frank Lawrence is shown on the right honoring an unidentified man with a Certificate of Appreciation and a star quilt. Frank was a former Chairman of the Standing Rock Sioux Tribe and is now deceased. (Undated photograph courtesy of Sitting Bull College.)

LEFT TO RIGHT: KEVIN WHITE BULL, JONATHAN PUTNAM, CLINT WALKER, AND LESLIE PUTNAM. These students are receiving awards. (Undated photograph courtesy of Sitting Bull College.)

POWWOW DANCING. The adults leading the children are Mary Louise Defender Wilson (Hunkpapa) and Arthur Amiotte (Oglala). The little dancers are unidentified. In the background standing by the stage are Tom Iron (Hunkpapa) in front and Wilbur "Banny Pleets (Hunkpapa). Mary is also a traditional storyteller and released a CD in 2001 entitled *My Relatives Say*. Arthur is a renowned artist and was an art instructor at Standing Rock Community College at this time. Tom Iron is a former Tribal Chairman of the Standing Rock Sioux Tribe and Wilbur works for the tribe today as a Contracting Officer. (Photo taken *c.* 1975, courtesy of Sitting Bull College.)

DUANE PHILLIPS AND ANN LEBEAU VALANDRA (STANDING ROCK). This photo was taken at Sitting Bull College while Duane and Ann are working at their jobs. Duane is from Wakpala, S.D. and Ann still works for the college as Director of the Job Placement and Training Program. (Photo taken in 1973, courtesy of Sitting Bull College.)

LEONARD BEAR KING (STANDING ROCK). Leonard Bear King was honored on two different years as the "Indian Educator of the Year." He is the uncle of Daryl No Heart and is from Kenel, S.D. Leonard is a veteran who served in the Korean War. (Undated photograph courtesy of Daryl No Heart.)

WAKPALA SIOUX MARCHING BAND. The Wakpala, S.D. High School marching band is shown here during a performance at Mobridge, S.D. next to the Mobridge City Park. (Undated photograph courtesy of Sitting Bull College.)

Nine

INYAN WOSLATA
(STANDING ROCK RESERVATION)
1954–2004

POWWOW GRAND ENTRY. Leading the Grand Entry are Kevin One Bull (with the American flag), Bob Montclair (with Albert Grass flag), Lavonnne Running Bear (to the left of the American flag), Rosa White Temple, Marie Many Wounds, Kathy Bailey, Carol Dwarf, Bessie Agard, and three unidentified children. Unfortunately some participants are hidden from view behind the flag, including the Powwow Queen, who is the daughter of Gladys Hawk. (Photo taken at Fort Yates, N.D., 1977, courtesy of Sitting Bull College.)

LILLIAN MARTINEZ (STANDING ROCK). Lillian Martinez, from Cannon Ball, N.D. is holding the microphone. The boy next to her is unidentified. In the background at far left are Hunkpapa members Isaac Dog Eagle and Cedric Goodhouse. (Photo taken *c.* 1975, courtesy of Sitting Bull College.)

SITTING BULL DESCENDANTS. This photo was taken during the dedication of a new grave location for Sitting Bull. Pictured from left to right are Margaret One Bull Tremmel, James White Bull, Nancy Stewart Kicking Bear, Claire ("Regina") One Bull-Spotted Horse, Clarence Grey Eagle, Sarah Little Spotted Horse, and Angeline Spotted Horse LaPointe. The three girls, Nancy, Sarah, and Angeline, gave Power of Attorney to Clarence for consent to move the body of Sitting Bull from Fort Yates to near Mobridge, S.D. Margaret, James, and Claire were signed witnesses. Nancy Stewart Kicking Bear's grandmother is Four Robes and her grandfather is Sitting Bull. Clarence Grey Eagle was the uncle of Sarah, Angeline, and Nancy. Clarence is the nephew of Sitting Bull's wives (Four Robes and Seen By Her Nation) by blood. Clarence's father was Grey Eagle and he was accused of betraying Sitting Bull when he was killed. Sarah and Angeline's grandparents are Seen By Her Nation and Sitting Bull. Although the descendants are from the Hunkpapa blood line, Nancy, Sarah, and Angeline all became enrolled with the Oglala's at Pine Ridge Indian Reservation because they moved there. James White Bull would be Minnicoujou/Hunkpapa and his father was White Bull, who was the brother of One Bull. Judy White Bull is one of the daughters of James White Bull whom the author has met with. Margaret One Bull Tremmel is the daughter of One Bull. One Bull was a nephew of Sitting Bull. Claire married Spotted Horse, and this Spotted Horse family is no relation to Urban Spotted Horse. Today, the One Bull and White Bull descendants would be great nephews or nieces of Sitting Bull. Today, Bill and Charlie Stewart (and their brothers and sisters) are grandsons of Nancy Stewart Kicking Bear, and Ernie LaPointe and Ethel Bates, children of Angeline Spotted Horse LaPointe are all well known by the author and as grandchildren of Sitting Bull have a direct family blood line to Sitting Bull. (Photo taken at Mobridge, S.D., April 1953, courtesy of Ernie LaPointe and Ethel Bates.)

VINE DELORIA, SR. Vine Deloria, Sr. was born at Wakpala, S.D. on October 6, 1901. His father was Rev. Philip Deloria, one of the first Sioux Episcopal priests, and his mother was the daughter of General Alfred Sully. Vine's grandfather was Saswe, a Yankton sub-chief and traditional religious leader of the White Swan Band. Vine Deloria, Sr. was ordained in 1932 and was assigned to Pine Ridge Mission. He also served at Rosebud and Sisseton-Wahpeton Reservations. He was an outstanding orator and storyteller who often used sports examples in his sermons, and he was among the first inductees of the South Dakota Hall of Fame. He died in Tucson, Arizona on February 26, 1990. (Undated photograph courtesy of South Dakota State Historical Society.)

DANCE CLUB. This photo is from the Little Eagle, S.D. Community Development book. The adult standing in the back is Frank White Buffalo Man. In the front row from left to right are Walter Chasing Hawk, Perry Bobtail Bear, Delbert Chasing Hawk, Charles Antelope, Shirley White Buffalo Man, Everette Chasing Hawk, Theodore Lawrence, and Richard Voorhees. (Photo taken 1955-56, courtesy of Ernestine Spotted Horse on behalf of her brother Charles Antelope and *Teton Times*.)

McLaughlin, S.D. Red Owl Store Staff. Pictured in the grocery store from left to right are: (standing) Al Sapa (District Manager), Philomene One Feather (produce), Patricia Poolaw (checker), Roberta Johnson (checker), Virginia McClain (produce), John Red Bear (Market Manager), Calvin Naasz (Store Manager), and Harold Culbertson (Executive Director of Standing Rock Enterprises); (front row) Tom Mentz (stock boy) and Lemoine Wiest (stock boy). (Undated photograph courtesy of *Teton Times*.)

Left to right: Doug Benway (Minnicoujou), Russell Benoist (Minnicoujou), Cordelia Flying Bye (Hunkpapa), Leona Hayes Flying Bye (Hunkpapa), Moses Flying Bye (Hunkpapa). This is a wedding day picture of the marriage of Russell Benoist and Cordelia Flying Bye, taken with their parents at the Congregational Church in Cherry Creek, S.D. on the Cheyenne River Reservation. (Photo taken at Cherry Creek, S.D., August 1959, courtesy of Mildred Benway.)

JOHN ARCHAMBAULT, BLANCHE J. ARCHAMBAULT VALANDRA, AND LOUIE ARCHAMBAULT (FRENCH-LAKOTA). The photo of these siblings was taken at Standing Rock *c.* 1960s–1970s. John Archambault and his wife Margaret Little Eagle were both born in 1892. They were the parents of Germaine Eagle and the grandparents of Sharon Archambault No Heart. Blanche Archambault married Louis Valandra and they had seven children. Blanche was born in 1895 and was nearing her 100th birthday when she died in 1995. Her parents were listed as Hermides "Harry" Archambault and Susan Black Elk. Louie Archambault married Annie Gates in 1902 at St. Peters Church at Fort Yates. (Photograph courtesy of Germain Eagle and Sharon No Heart.)

LEFT TO RIGHT: PETER RED TOMAHAWK, EDNA WINDY, FRANCIS RED TOMAHAWK, AND FLORENCE MELVIN (HUNKPAPA). Peter and Edna were the parents of Brenda Red Tomahawk. Francis "Putchie" and Florence are her uncle and auntie. Peter is holding a rooster chicken. (Undated photograph courtesy of Brenda Red Tomahawk.)

ANGELINE SPOTTED HORSE LaPOINTE AND ERNIE LaPOINTE. Angeline is the Granddaughter of Sitting Bull, pictured here with her son Ernie at their home. Angeline and Ernie were both born at Pine Ridge and are enrolled at Pine Ridge instead of at Standing Rock. Angeline was born in 1903 and her mother was Mary Sitting Bull (Standing Holy), who was born in Montana in 1876. Mary's mother was Seen By Her Nation, wife of Sitting Bull. Seen By Her Nation was born in 1846 and Sitting Bull was born in March of 1831. Ernie is the great grandson of Sitting Bull. (Photo taken at Oglala, S.D., c. 1953, courtesy of Ernie LaPointe and Ethel Bates.)

LEFT TO RIGHT: ERNESTINE (RED TOMAHAWK) HURAVITCH, BRENDA RED TOMAHAWK, KATHLEEN (RED TOMAHAWK) VETTER (HUNKPAPA). This photo of these three sisters was taken at Breien, N.D., with their sunka. Ernestine is the tallest, Kathleen is wearing the white dress, and Brenda is in the stroller. (Photo taken c. 1959, courtesy of Brenda Red Tomahawk.)

114

ANGELINE SPOTTED HORSE LAPOINTE (HUNKPAPA). Angeline is dressed in traditional style at their first house after leaving the Pine Ridge Indian Reservation. Her parents were Spotted Horse, born in 1873, and Mary Sitting Bull, born in Montana in 1876. Chief Sitting Bull was Angeline's Grandfather. The car was a mint green 1951 Pontiac. (Photo taken at Rapid City, S.D., 1957, courtesy of Ernie LaPointe and Ethel Bates.)

AGARD FAMILY (STANDING ROCK). This is believed to be the Agard Family. Pictured from left to right are Cindy Agard, Aljoe Agard, Bessie Agard, and Alvina Agard. The family is demonstrating the Lakota method of cooking by using animal skins filled with water, and adding heated rocks for boiling. Aljoe was a former Tribal Chairman and he holds a canumpa (pipe). (Photo taken by Mohr, Mandan, N.D., courtesy of Brenda Red Tomahawk.)

FRONT ROW, LEFT TO RIGHT: DAVE LUGER, BERNARD "SATCH" STANDING CROW, AND LEO CHASING HAWK. The others are unidentified. Bernard "Satch" Standing Crow was a long-time Judge for the Standing Rock Sioux Tribe and a nephew of his is Earl Bull Head. (Undated photo courtesy of Sitting Bull College.)

STANDING ROCK TRIBAL COUNCIL AT FORT YATES, N.D. Pictured from left to right are: (back row) Pete Taken Alive, two unidentified, Guy Shooting Bear, Harry Swift Horse, Aljoe Agard, James McLain, and Attorney Marvin Sonosky; (middle row) Joe Condon, Sr. (with white tie) and Charles Gabe, Sr. (with dark shirt and pen in shirt pocket); (front row) Dave Black Cloud, Ted "Tiny Bud" Jamerson, Pete Red Dog. This photo was found in the tribal archives. (Undated photograph courtesy of *Teton Times* and Standing Rock Sioux Tribe.)

JOHN GREY EAGLE (STANDING), ELAINE GREY EAGLE ARCHAMBAULT (HOLDING ONE OF HER DAUGHTERS) (STANDING ROCK). John Grey Eagle is the father of Elaine Grey Eagle. John was born in 1898 and married Cecelia Thief of Kenel, S.D. A brother of Cecelia is Louie Thief, also from Kenel. The parents of John Grey Eagle were Samuel Grey Eagle (born in 1874) and Annie Brave Thunder (born in 1870). Elaine married Edgar Archambault and they had ten children, including Sharon Archambault No Heart, who provided the photo. Edgar's sister is Germaine Eagle of Bullhead, S.D. (Photo taken at Minneapolis, MN May 1961, courtesy of Germaine Eagle and Sharon No Heart.)

LEO HALSEY. Leo Halsey of Fort Yates takes a break from his work at the college in this photo. (Photo taken at Standing Rock Community College, 1979, courtesy of Sitting Bull College.)

OLIVER EAGLEMAN (HUNKPAPA).
Oliver lives in the community of
Wakpala, S.D. and is 82 years old.
This picture was taken when he was
visiting Crazy Horse Memorial in the
Black Hills of South Dakota. (Undated
photo taken at Crazy Horse, S.D.,
courtesy of Charmayne Eagleman.)

**VINE DELORIA, JR. (YANKTON/STANDING
ROCK).** Vine Deloria, Jr. is the author of
many books of American Indian policy
and history. His well known early books
include *Custer Died For Your Sins, Behind
The Trail Of Broken Treaties,* and *God Is Red.*
He was born in Martin, S.D. to Vine, Sr.
and Barbara Eastman Deloria. Vine's great
grandfather was Francois Des Laurias ("Saswe")
who was a medicine man and leader of the
White Swan Band of the Yankton Sioux
tribe. Phillip Deloria, priest of the Episcopal
Church at Wakpala, was Vine Deloria Jr.'s
grandfather and Ella C. Deloria was an aunt
of Vine's. Vine Deloria, Jr. served as the
Executive Director of the National Congress
of American Indians (NCAI) from 1964-1967,
and also held many other prestigious positions.
The author had the opportunity in 1994 to
re-introduce Vine at his former alma mater,
Iowa State University, when the author worked
for the Iowa Regents Universities. Vine is
now a retired Professor from the University
of Colorado at Boulder. He also has a law
degree and a degree in theology. (Photo taken,
c. 1970, courtesy of Sitting Bull College.)

LEVI WAGGONER (HUNKPAPA). Levi was the son of John Franklin (J.F.) Waggoner and Josephine McCarty Waggoner. Levi was an enrolled member of the tribe who was born on April 8, 1899 at Fort Yates, N.D. and passed away in October, 1995 at the age of 96. Both of his parents were well known. Josephine was a historian, and J.F. Waggoner was a U.S. cavalry soldier for 22 years and was with Captain Benteen at the Battle of the Little Bighorn. He was later a cattleman, and built the first Catholic Church at Fort Yates and also built a Catholic Church south of McLaughlin. He also built the coffin for Sitting Bull and was in charge of his burial. He was unhappy that a decision was made to put quicklime on the body of Sitting Bull. People said they dug up the bones of Sitting Bull as early as 1905 but Mr. Waggoner said the actual grave site was 100 yards away from this dig. Levi's mother Josephine was the daughter of Charles McCarty, a member of the Shoot The Bear family from near Wakpala. Josephine was the author of several books including *Rekindling The Campfires*. Levi was the oldest boy and had three brothers and five sisters. Levi attended Carlisle Indian School in Pennsylvania and was a classmate of the Olympian, Jim Thorpe. Levi was also a musician and played in Robert Bruce's band from Selfridge, N.D. (Undated photograph courtesy of Chester Fuhrman.)

MARGUERITE MEDICINE FIDDLER (SIHA SAPA). This photo of Marguerite is at a powwow and they are viewing the activities. A sister of Marguerite's is Bea Medicine. (Photo taken at Fort Yates, N.D., *c.* 1975, courtesy of Sitting Bull College.)

CHIEF'S RIDE. This is the 4th Annual Chief's Ride which was organized by Sitting Bull College members, Robert Gipp, President of the Board of Trustees, and Ron His Horse Is Thunder, President of Sitting Bull College. The ride is to honor past Chief's and leaders. (Photograph courtesy of Linda Sharff.)

CULTURAL PRESENTATION. This was a cultural presentation in a school gymnasium. At the far left in front of the tipi are Lavonne Agard, Evelyn Agard, and Bernice Agard-Claymore. This photo was found in the tribal archives at Fort Yates. (Photo taken c. 1950, courtesy of Teton Times and Standing Rock Sioux Tribe.)

THERESA TALLEY. Theresa "Terri" Talley of Kenel, SD is pictured on the left facing the camera while dancing at Fort Yates, N.D. (Undated Photograph courtesy of Sitting Bull College.)

ETHEL BATES (HUNKPAPA) AND DONOVIN SPRAGUE (MINNICOUJOU). The author is pictured here with Ethel Bates, who is the great granddaughter of Chief Sitting Bull and his wife Seen By Her Nation. Ethel's parents were Allison Little Spotted Horse and Angeline Spotted Horse. Ethel was born at Oglala, S.D. on Pine Ridge Reservation and her sisters are Marlene Andersen and Lydia Red Paint. Her brother is Ernie LaPointe. Ethel is married to Scott Bates. The picture was taken on Native American Day at Crazy Horse Memorial in the Black Hills of South Dakota. The area of the room they are standing in honors Sitting Bull. The author is the great great grandson of Chief Hump of the Minnicoujou. Both Hump and Sitting Bull allied their bands in the same area in Alberta and Saskatchewan, Canada, and both leaders participated at the Battle of Little Big Horn. (Photo taken at Crazy Horse, S.D. on Oct. 13, 2003, courtesy of Donovin Sprague.)

LEFT TO RIGHT: DELBERT CHASING HAWK, CHIEF TWO BEARS III (YANKTONAI), AND EVERETT CHASING HAWK. There were two different Two Bear families. Chief Two Bears III was the last survivor of the White Horse Riders. President Grant presented Two Bears with a peace medal and a horse. He is shown leading a war dance at a powwow. (Undated photo taken by Mohr, Bismarck, N.D., courtesy of Brenda Red Tomahawk.)

122

KEVIN LOCKE "TOKEYA INAJIN" ("THE FIRST TO ARRIVE") (LAKOTA). Kevin is a renowned flute and hoop dance performer. He is a recording artist for Makoce Records of Bismarck, N.D. Kevin is also a university graduate and educator of both Lakota and non-Indian cultures. He was awarded a National Heritage Fellowship by the National Endowment for the Arts in 1990. He is shown here performing the hoop dance. Kevin lives in Wakpala, SD with his wife Dorothy, daughters Kimimila and Waniya, and son Ohiyesa. (Photo by Bruce Wendt, courtesy of Makoce Recording Company.)

MARY LOUISE DEFENDER WILSON "GOURD WOMAN" (DAKOTA). Mary Louise is a traditional storyteller on Standing Rock Reservation. She learned stories from her mother Helen Margaret See The Bear and from her grandmother. The stories were to educate children and adults. She is a recipient of a National Heritage Fellowship from the National Endowment for the Arts. She has recorded her stories onto CD for Makoce Records of Bismarck, N.D. and has received a Native American Music Award for Best Spoken Word Recording, the National Education Association's H. Council Trenholm Memorial Award for Human and Civil Rights, and a Notable Document Award from the Government Documents Round Table of the American Library Association. She was the first Miss Indian America in 1954 and she married William Dean. (Photo by Dennis Gad, courtesy of Makoce Recording Company.)

DARYL AND SHARON NO HEART (HUNKPAPA). The buffalo robe was painted by artist Daryl No Heart and is now displayed in the Fort Yates, N.D. High School Auditorium. Mr. and Mrs. No Heart have a printing business, Wico Hunkake, in Rapid City, S.D. (Photo taken at Minneapolis, MN in 1994, courtesy of Daryl and Sharon No Heart.)

SISSY GOODHOUSE (STANDING ROCK). Sissy Goodhouse performs traditional olowan (music) with her family. The Goodhouse family record for Makoce Records, Bismarck, N.D. The grandfathers of Sissy are Joe Flying Bye and Henry Swift Bird, and the grandmother of Sissy is Helen Shell Track, all of whom she credits for her musical direction of her place and purpose at the drum. (Photo by Makoce, courtesy of Makoce Recording Company.)

PATRICIA LOCKE "TA WACIN WASTE WIN"
(HUNKPAPA/CHIPPEWA). Patricia Locke has received
numerous awards in education and is credited with
assisting 17 tribes in establishing Indian community
colleges on their reservations. She taught at UCLA, and
was the author of 29 articles and publications. (Undated
photograph courtesy of Winona Flying Earth.)

STANDING ROCK SIOUX TRIBAL ADMINISTRATION BUILDING. This is the new tribal headquarters
of the Standing Rock Sioux Tribe at Fort Yates, N.D. where administration affairs is housed,
including the office of Tribal Chairman Charles Murphy. The building was dedicated at a grand
opening held on June 30, 2003. The reservation was established on March 2, 1889. The tribe also
has two gambling casinos; Prairie Knights Casino near Cannon Ball and the Grand River Casino
between Wakpala and Mobridge. (Photo taken in 2003, courtesy of Donovin Sprague.)

INDEX

BIBLIOGRAPHY

Carlisle Indian School Records, Carlisle, Pennsylvania.

Corson County History book staff. *Corson County History, South Dakota*

Deloria, Ella C. *Dakota Texts*. 1932.

Densmore, Frances. *Teton Sioux Music and Dance*. University of Nebraska: Lincoln and London. 1918.

Hampton Institute School Records, Hampton, Virginia.

Hedron, Paul L. *Sitting Bull's Surrender at Fort Buford*. Fort Union Association, Williston, North Dakota. 1997.

Lewis and Clark Journals.

Sioux County History book staff. *Sioux County History*. Selfridge, North Dakota.

Sprague, Donovin. *Cheyenne River Sioux*. Arcadia Publishing, Chicago, IL 2003.

Visit us at
arcadiapublishing.com